SWITCH

WORDS

HOW TO USE **ONE WORD** TO GET WHAT YOU WANT

LIZ DEAN

Thorsons

The contents of this book should be used as a general guideline only. Nothing in this book should be taken as medical advice or diagnosis, and you should always consult with a qualified medical practitioner before starting any health programme or if you have any concerns about your health. The author and the publishers do not accept any responsibility for any loss or harm that may occur from your use or misuse of this book or your failure to seek appropriate medical advice.

Reasonable efforts have been made to contact relevant rights owners of material included in this book. Such persons are invited to contact us.

Thorsons
An imprint of HarperCollins*Publishers*
1 London Bridge Street
London SE1 9GF

www.harpercollins.co.uk

First published by Thorsons 2015

A catalogue record of this book is available
from the British Library

ISBN 978-0-00-814423-4

Printed and bound in Great Britain by
CPI Group (UK) Ltd, Croydon CR0 4YY

Contents

Contents

How to use this book

Ever wanted to make fast changes to your life? Bring in more money, increase your potential for success, reach for a brilliant idea, write a book, create a business, lose weight, study more effectively, speak in public, pass your driving test, heal emotional patterns or just find an item you've lost?

You can do this with one word: a Switchword. You can achieve what you've set your heart on without meditating, adopting a radical belief system or spending hours learning online. Switchwords are uniquely chosen words that switch on your subconscious. They 'flip a switch' in your beliefs and behaviour at a deep level. They bring you together so you can attract what you want in life. Like waving a magic wand, speaking, thinking or chanting these words connects you completely with the goals you desire – and brings them to you.

The Introduction and Chapter 1 explain the principles: why Switchwords work, and what they can do for you. In Chapter 2, discover the easy techniques: how to say, think or chant your word, how to make a Switchword phrase and how to muscle-test the words that are 'strong' for you. If you want to try Switchwording right away, check into Chapter 3 and see the magic words that can empower every area of your life, from relationships to career-building, creativity to health. There's also a 'Seven Ways' plan to demonstrate how to use Switchwords throughout the day, whether you're travelling into work or trying to get to sleep. There is, literally, one word for everything.

Next, find your personal Switchwords in Chapter 4, or delve into Chapter 5 to discover the words for physical, emotional and spiritual wellbeing and healing. Chapter 6 gives you further ways to use Switchwords, combining them with tapping (also known as Emotional Freedom Techniques – EFTs) and neuro-linguistic programming (NLP). The Dictionary in the Appendix lists over 200 Switchwords, from A to Z – any time you need inspiration to find a Switchword, flick through the Dictionary pages, stop where you want and choose a word.

Throughout the book there are case studies – illustrating how people from every walk of life have used Switchwords to benefit their finances, lower their anxiety levels, improve their confidence and boost their success – along with tips and exercises to try.

Your life can change now – with one word.

I hope this book will be the start of your journey into Switchwords, and that you receive the love, money, success, confidence and better health you deserve.

Introduction:
Open Sesame!

A woodcutter named Ali Baba chanced upon a dozen men making their way through the forest. Afraid they were robbers, he climbed into a tree. Their leader called out, 'Open sesame!' and there opened a portal in the rocks into which all the men entered. The door shut behind them. After some time, the forty men emerged, all laden with goods. 'Shut sesame!' the captain called, and he closed the door, then he and his men turned back through the forest.

The woodcutter, from his tree, thought about what he had seen. He and his family had little food and no money, despite his brother, Cassim, who was wealthy but mean. So, remembering the magic words, Ali Baba approached the door in the rocks and called out, 'Open sesame!' On entering through the door, he found a vault of glittering treasure: gold coins, overflowing pearls and piles of precious jewels. He took all the gold he could carry, called 'Shut sesame!' and closed the door.

Paraphrased from *Ali Baba and the Forty Thieves*

'Open sesame', 'hey presto', 'abracadabra': your wish is granted. Wouldn't it be wonderful if words could really do this? Well, they can, and these miraculous words are known as Switchwords. These powerful declarations switch on the subconscious mind, helping you to manifest what you want in life. Forming a verbal code that the subconscious understands, Switchwords act immediately to align the subconscious mind with our conscious intention. When we are together with ourselves, aligned and resonating – completely 'switched on' – we are truly in possession of our own power, able to attract what we want in life. These power-words work more effectively than conscious affirmations (see page xv); they work in much the same way as mantras – the sound vibrations of the words, which are often not literal requests, affect the universal energy around us, so we become not only aligned within ourselves, but with a benevolent universe that can grant our wishes. In this way, Switchwords are a form of manifesting based on the Law of Attraction (see page xii): like attracts like. Put out a positive, authentic wish to the universe, and it is really possible to receive it – with just one word.

We use common words as 'switches' to open doors every day. Just as Ali Baba learned that 'open sesame' was the magic formula that unlocked the vault of treasures, the simple 'please' and 'thank you' were the magic words of our childhoods. 'Say the magic word,' we would be instructed in order to get what we wanted, whether it was a Christmas present, a piece of cake or the permission to play with a toy. Parents and other caregivers constantly set these magic words as a test, in the knowledge that we will need them to traverse the paths of communication as adults – please in order to get, thank you in order to politely receive. Like 'please', a Switchword is the 'get' word of magic, getting the subconscious and the universe onside so we can manifest whatever we choose – without meditation, guilt or bargaining.

The manifesting magic of words is seeded in the translation of the magician's favourite, 'abracadabra', from the Aramaic *avra kehdabra*, 'I create as I speak' or 'I create like the word'; in Hebrew, it may come from a phrase meaning, 'It came to pass as it was spoken.' The earliest written evidence of 'abracadabra' is the 2nd-century medical poem *De medicina praecepta* by the Roman physician Quintus Serenus Sammonicus, who recommended the word be written in the shape of an inverted triangle, beginning with 'abracadabra' on the first line, then for every line under it one letter from the end of the word was dropped, leaving just the first 'a' at the point of the triangle. Worn as an amulet to cure disease, the funnel shape of the words symbolised sickness being drawn downwards out of the body, vanishing into nothing; as if by magic, the illness would disappear. The magic words we associate with conjurors, like Switchwords, are used to make something appear or disappear, to access a special place or to magically transform reality – words are the passwords between this world and another realm. 'Hocus pocus' has its origins in the Latin phrase *hoc est corpus*, recited as part of the Eucharist when the wine and bread become the blood and body of Christ, signifying the magical transformation of matter from one form to another. Ali Baba's 'open sesame' may translate as 'heaven, open'. Switchwords, as you will see, are our magic key to opening up a whole world of possibilities.

The Three Switchwords You Need to Know Now

Here are the 'manifesting' Switchwords to bring you what you want:

TOGETHER – The 'master' Switchword for everything

DIVINE – Asks for a miracle

DIVINE ORDER – Helps you do anything efficiently and restores order from chaos

BRING – Brings you whatever you ask for

What can Switchwords do for me?

Switchwords can benefit all aspects of your life, from work and creative projects to relationships and finances (see Chapter 3, which gives Switchwords by life area, on page 37). Here are just some of the benefits.

Switchwords can:

- Help deal with pain, low mood and stress-related ailments
- Support efforts to break negative habits
- Promote sleep and peace of mind
- Help problem-solve, and inspire creativity
- Boost leadership qualities
- Manifest money
- Attract love and friendship
- Deepen existing relationship bonds
- Assist education and study
- Support healing
- Combine with existing therapies such as Reiki and NLP

Although, as with any other therapy, Switchwords cannot claim to cure illness or take away pain, working with these words has led to a reduction in symptoms for some people, and helped them manage their pain and associated low mood more confidently and effectively. There are also many empowering Switchwords, to boost leadership qualities, bring courage, and engender happiness and calm. While we cannot be happy all of the time, we can adjust how we deal with difficult circumstances.

The case studies throughout this book give examples of exactly how people with a range of experiences have used Switchwords to turn negatives into positives and receive what they need in life.

How do Switchwords work?

Switchwords operate through vibration. Saying, intending or chanting these words of power changes our body's vibration so that we resonate at the same frequency as the goal we desire. When we say, intend, chant or sing Switchwords we create sympathetic resonance and attract what we want. According to the Law of Attraction, like attracts like. When our thoughts, words, actions and beliefs become what we aspire to, we attract this to us like a magnet. The Law of Attraction, a philosophical movement that emerged in the early 1900s, is the foundation of the international bestseller *The Secret* by Rhonda Byrne (see the Appendix, page 128).

'Words can be like X-rays if you use them properly – they'll go through anything.'
ALDOUS HUXLEY

When Switchwords are intended through thought, speech, chanting or singing, a vibration is created. Sound healer Petra Galligan describes Switchwords as an echo – a sound that reverberates after the initial sound has stopped. The energy pattern created by the word's sound vibration continues – and so the Switchword replicates itself. This idea of replication through sound is embedded in Richard Dawkins's concept of the 'meme'. Meaning 'to imitate', memes are ideas or agents of culture that self-propagate like genes, transmitting from brain to brain through the senses. Sound memes, such as melodies and catchphrases, are transmitted through pronunciation. Like a virus, a meme can be considered a living organism that spreads beyond the speaker through replication. If we consider that Switchwords are a type of sound meme, it follows that when we use Switchwords we send out a vibration through sound that communicates beyond the self, creating an environment that is aligned with our purpose, bringing the desired result.

The Switchword COPY resonates with Dawkins's meme theory, as it's recited to manifest pregnancy – in other words, to continue a genetic lineage. To copy is to replicate; to repeat the word COPY is to continue the replication of cells.

When we repeat Switchwords there's also a shift in the brain. Our attention shifts from the word to the sound of the word, the meaning then falls away and you have just the vibration. This is known as semantic satiation. Have you noticed that when you look at a word over and over again it begins to appear less meaningful? Run your eye over words you've added to a Scrabble board (or cast your mind back to writing 100 lines of 'I will not talk in class' at school) and the words seem to melt into a pattern of shapes. They are simply form and sound – vibrational objects. This is why it doesn't matter if you don't understand why particular words act as Switches – we do not need to make a link between the semantics and the effect. The effect is created by the sound and feel of the word, which then aligns your energy to manifest your goal.

Switchwords as mantras – the vibration of transformation

The power of words to transform reality through sound vibration is illustrated by mantras (the word 'mantra' derives from Sanskrit, a vibrational language, and means 'instrument of thought'). If we accept the loose definition that a mantra is a melodic pattern of words repeated to bring about a change in consciousness, reciting a mantra aims to create an altered reality. This is an important concept in Switchwording: the idea that spoken words can be transformational, creating an effect outside of the self, is funda-mental to the belief that they will work and manifest a chosen desire. Once spoken and repeated as a mantra, a Switchword gains its own momentum. A Sufi saying states, 'You stop doing the mantra, and the mantra starts doing you.' In other words, the mantra manifests your intention, and it comes back to you as an experience. Words, thoughts and beliefs, recited with intention, create reality.

Sanskrit scholar Dr Douglas Brooks comments, 'Sanskrit tells us what Nature shows us. A limited number of rules gives an arbitrarily large number of outcomes. The way Nature goes about its business, Sanskrit goes about its language.' This reference to 'a limited number of rules gives an arbitrarily large number of outcomes' is suggestive of chaos theory and the butterfly effect proposed by the American mathematician and meteorologist Edward Lorenz. The theory, in very simple terms, is that one subtle event in one part of the world can effect a greater change elsewhere. The energy generated by the subtle movement of a butterfly wing potentially results in a tornado on the other side of the world. As a mantra is action and intention, it activates the energy of the universe, which responds in kind, bringing to us an event, a realisation or an experience greater in energy than the energy of the original intention. A single word, repeated, may bring us much more than an echo of the word. It brings us a result that is a tangible expression of our desire.

Why 10, 28 or 108 chants?

You can say a Switchword as a mantra by simply repeating it as often as you like, or you can go for the traditional numbers of chant in mantra, which are 10, 28 or 108. The number 108 is sacred in Vedic philosophy. There are 108 Upanishads, and 108 is the number of steps from the material world to that of the divine in Hindu and Buddhist traditions. There are also 108 names of Shiva, the Hindu destroyer-god, and 108 volumes of the Kangyur ('The Translation of the Word'), the Tibetan sacred text that is believed to contain the words of the Buddha himself. The popular recitation of mantras 108 or 28 times (among other numbers) may also derive from the sacred

Sanskrit Gayatri Mantra, a verse from the hymn of the Rigveda, which dates from around 1500–1200 BCE. The Gayatri Mantra is repeated 10, 18, 28, 108 or 1,000 times for the chanter's spiritual development and to bring him what he wants in life. Mariasusai Dhavamony in *Classical Hinduism* explains, 'It [the Gayatri Mantra] not only serves the purpose of concentrating the mind on the divine object, but also confers on the reciters the "mystical" power and the fulfilment of his desires ...'

Why Switchwords succeed where affirmations can fail

The difference between Switchwording and affirmations lies in the part of the brain that they're designed to address. Switchwords work through sound and feel, which creates a vibration that speaks to the unconscious mind; affirmations work through semantics, or the words' meanings, which has a direct appeal to the conscious mind. Affirmations use words that exactly match our purpose ('I am strong, I am successful'), whereas Switchwords reach behind the conscious brain to get to the part that affirmations do not reach. Does our unconscious mind truly believe 'I am strong, I am successful' yet? Often, there's a part of us that's decrying the affirmation – the cynical 'Oh yeah' voice within that's yet to be convinced that we could be anything other than we are. Also, there's a scientific reason why our positive, conscious affirmations often don't get through. According to Mark Waldman and Andrew Newberg MD, 'The brain barely responds to our positive words and thoughts. They're not a threat to our survival, so the brain doesn't need to respond as rapidly as it does to negative thoughts and words.' The part of the brain that responds to threats to our survival ('fight or flight' mode, as it is known) is the amygdala, which plays a role in the unconscious memory. Perhaps the amygdala, the old, reptilian part of the brain, is involved in the response to Switchwords, resulting in a decrease in or deletion of negative memories that can drive our actions and decisions. If we try to manifest what we want in life when old memories and beliefs oppose our conscious willingness, it's likely that our wishes won't produce results. Switchwords align us so that we can manifest. This is why TOGETHER is the master Switchword (see page 38), because it brings us into perfect alignment within ourselves and attunes us to the universe.

Because Switchwords are not literal, they slip under the radar of the conscious mind without revealing their purpose. That way, the conscious mind can't intervene, question, analyse or disrupt their flow. It can't hinder the flow of energy or block our ability to manifest. For example, the affirmation 'I take positive action' has just that literal meaning. The universal Switchword for the same effect is: NOW.

Take the Switchword SUFFER. Its meaning is to manage prosperity – so SUFFER is quite the opposite of what we would get with an affirmation (such as 'My life is filled with abundance'). This doesn't mean you can't continue to use your positive affirmations if you want to – they can be very helpful in reinforcing your integrity in stressful situations – but, in my experience, Switchwords work more quickly and more profoundly.

For this reason, Switchwords appear to have more in common with mantras than with positive affirmations. As Switchwords work through vibrational rather than literal meaning, they share their purpose with mantras – the first mantras were constructed according to their sound, rooted in the seed syllable 'Om' or *pranava*, meaning 'sound' and 'humming'. An affirmation may have a sound or vibrational aspect – such as rhyme, assonance or alliteration ('Beat the others to be the best'; 'What you resist persists') – yet these effects are often secondary, intended only as an *aide-mémoire*. Again, with Switchwords we don't need to understand the words, know them or have any personal point of reference for them to work. They operate on the vibration of sound, rather than the anchor of conscious knowing. Philosopher Frits Staal (1930–2012), who did not believe that the words of mantras had much literal meaning, compared them to birdsong. While we may not understand the language, we acknowledge it as a form of communication through sound.

Believe it or not ... Switchwords work

Believing that your Switchwords will work and trusting that what you've wished for will be delivered gives energy to your manifesting, but even with minimal belief these amazing words still appear to work. Here's just one example.

The morning after I sent out my regular Switchword email to my group, two recipients immediately replied. They had won exactly the same amount of money after chanting the Switch phrases 'FIND-DIVINE-COUNT-ON' and 'ELOHIM-DIVINE', which I'd included in my email for the first time. The response from Jon, a teacher who was curious about my interests rather than enamoured, was the first to ping into my inbox. I'd included him on my mailing list because he's a friend and I knew he could do with more cash. He wrote, 'I did it [FIND-DIVINE-COUNT-ON] in a rather cynical way and got a £25 payout on premium bonds today!' He's now working with REACH to find a long-lost book. Next was Rhonda's email. Rhonda is a kindred spirit who thoroughly believes in angels and manifesting. She chose ELOHIM-DIVINE as her Switch-pair, which asks for a miracle from God or the universe. Plagued by money worries for months, she wrote: 'Liz, I won £25 on yesterday's Lotto!! Most I've ever won. Started playing two months ago. Do you think it's the Switchword working already? Last night I repeated it 28 times. I am on the train to work feeling very wealthy!'

Perhaps Jon's lack of attachment to the outcome actually helped him; he was willing to be open-minded and try, and he received a small reward as a result. Perhaps Rhonda's total belief helped her; she was dedicated to her Switchword practice and it paid off. Whichever, it doesn't matter. Two very different people had exactly the same result after chanting their Switchwords, and the universe responded regardless of their level of belief. All you need is the belief that it's worth trying: the universe takes care of the rest. What do you have to lose?

Ellen, firmly in Jon's sceptical camp, shared her story with me: 'I was looking for a gardening book and I'd searched everywhere. Then your email arrived and I used REACH to find it (although I was sceptical). I set a time limit of that day and when it didn't turn up, I felt my scepticism was justified. However, the following day I was walking past a bookcase that I had already searched through, and there it was. Did the same with a mislaid bicycle pump and found it almost straight away. Scepticism overruled (for now!)'

While a successful track record obviously helps belief (the more we succeed, the more we trust in the process), research also suggests that familiarity *alone* generates positive thoughts. Even if we're only able to carry the basic belief that Switchwords are worth trying – but don't necessarily believe that they will work – we cultivate belief as a by-product. This is known as the exposure effect. We have positive thoughts about things we've seen or heard (or experienced through other senses) before. This is true, of course, in advertising (which is why we're bombarded with repeated adverts) and also in music. A refrain or chorus has the effect of enchanting the brain – the exposure effect of repetition means we come to like what we're familiar with. So this is part of the belief factor in Switchwords: the more familiar we become with the Switchwords we choose, the more we generate an inner belief that they will work, whether we're conscious of this or not.

💡 **Tip:** Use CARE to remember the parts of this book you need.

There's a Switchword to help you store information – including Switchwords. This word is CARE. You might imagine this as the 'save' function on a computer. CARE helps you bank information for retrieval later. Whenever you pause in your reading of this book, say, think or chant the Switchword CARE to help you store the information you need. When you want to remember a Switchword or any part of this book later on, use the 'finding' Switchword REACH, which retrieves whatever you need, when you need it.

Ready for the next step?

1

Working with Switchwords

Opening the pathways to success

The subconscious houses that aspect of our higher self (or super-consciousness) that can be thought of as the guiding principle that wants what is best for us in this lifetime, attracting the wise lessons we need to learn, and inspiring us to act from a place of love rather than fear. When we use Switchwords, we are switching on the subconscious and the higher self to bring us what we genuinely need (rather than what the ego, expressed through the conscious mind, assumes we should have).

The subconscious mind holds thoughts, impressions and beliefs that the conscious mind is not aware of. These hidden attitudes have a powerful effect on our lives, both positive and negative, whether we achieve or fail, falter or procrastinate, take risks or confront problems. Your subconscious mind can be your greatest ally in achievement. It responds to the energy of the thoughts and feelings within you to attract external influences that hold the same vibration: like attracts like. This is the basis of manifesting – the belief that we can change our reality by changing our thoughts.

So, while we tell ourselves what we'd like to achieve, we also assume that our subconscious mind hears the command, understands it, believes in our missions and enters wholly into the agreement. Our beliefs, actions and words are consistent with the goal we'd like to achieve – or so we assume. We think we're together as one, a perfect union of the conscious and subconscious self, all geared up to make whatever we want happen.

Experience, however, shows us that this isn't always so, and we're often left bewildered by our failure to complete a task or make a substantial change in our lives. When our subconscious mind appears to ignore or even sabotage our conscious desire through action or inaction, it's virtually impossible to create and sustain the new reality we want, whether it's making more money or beginning a new business, managing time, dealing with anxiety and fear or breaking negative habits.

If we need more money, we might consciously affirm, 'I am wealthy, I live in abundance,' and repeat this on a daily basis, often reciting it while looking at ourselves in a mirror and imagining how we'd feel if we were rich and successful. But what if our under-lying belief conflicts with this affirmation? What if, at some level, we don't believe we deserve – or want – money?

Liam's money

Here's an example. Liam lost his father when he was 26 years old; they had been very close. His mother had passed away when he was just five years old, and Liam was now devastated at the loss of his sole parent. The proceeds from the sale of his father's home were then divided between him and his brother, Patrick. Liam was not wealthy – he earned a modest wage – and willingly accepted the money from the house proceeds.

But this is what happened next. Liam immediately spent £35,000 on home improvements. He and his wife, Sarah, had been trying to sell their house for 18 months in a slow market, and Liam believed this would make it saleable. It was way more than they needed to spend, but he insisted. Why spend so much on a house they were going to leave, Sarah asked?

A friend Liam worked with needed a heart operation. She would have to wait eight months for surgery, until Liam offered her £9,000 so she could have her operation within weeks.

Another friend ran a breast cancer charity. He donated £5,000.

He spent £10,000 on a better car, but sold it within three months. He didn't like the steering.

And then all the inheritance money was gone. When their house finally sold, its price had only increased by a fraction of the value of the improvements.

Looking back on that period of his life, Liam reflected: 'How could I have spent that money on myself? It was Dad's money … It somehow didn't feel right.'

Sarah added: 'That money was contaminated for him, so he took no pleasure in it. He maybe had the feeling it was right to suffer emotionally and financially – not to benefit. So, in effect, he gave it away.'

Liam's grief over his father got expressed through money – he got rid of it as quickly as he could, making sure not to purchase anything he would have to live with long-term. A subconscious money programme was running the show, not his conscious mind, which knew, logically, that the money should be spent first to help himself and his family (with donations secondary). This was how he consciously chose to spend his inheritance. But his true beliefs about what the legacy money meant showed up in his actions. He made decisions about spending from a place outside of his immediate conscious awareness.

So how did Liam's actions get ahead of his conscious decision not to spend money in the way he spent it? One explanation is that …

The subconscious has impeccable timing

One aspect of the drive of subconscious behaviour is its timing; there's a race between the subconscious urge and the conscious reaction. Say you want to kick your eBay habit – browsing and buying has become all too consuming; you know you're spending too much time and money, but yet again you drift onto the site after an email leads you to Facebook, which somehow reminds you that you *could* just take a peek at eBay. No harm done yet. Your conscious mind senses that you're about to break your own rule, but you're in the thrill of the danger zone, directed by that old subconscious urge. You click and buy (after all, it's already happening, so it's too late). The reason why the hand gets to the mouse before the conscious mind can effectively intervene might be explained by neuroscientist Heather A. Berlin: 'Recent imaging, psychophysical and neuropsychological findings suggest that unconscious processes take place hundreds of milliseconds before conscious awareness.' Could this be the neurological reason why our subconscious wins out, why it's always one step ahead? This is brilliant news if we have self-togetherness and self-awareness; the knowing, clever subconscious takes action before we get too analytical, and gets the job done. But if you're subject to negative habits, which are deeply ingrained in the subconscious, the subconscious wins again, and sabotages our goal.

Liam's subconscious behaviour pattern is also illuminated by research conducted by various cognitive neuroscientists. Studies suggest that the conscious mind is only in control around 5 per cent of the time, whereas the programmes of the subconscious mind influence 95 per cent or more of our experiences. This is a stunning statistic; in effect, we're run by our subconscious programmes most of the time. Which is fine if enough of our programming is positive, but if not – and rarely do we have dominantly positive programming

– the results can be failure and frustration. Just as Freud believed that we are driven by our subconscious patterning, the biologist Bruce Lipton in his book *The Biology of Belief* comments:

> ... We are completely unaware that our subconscious minds are making our everyday decisions. Our lives are essentially a printout of our subconscious programmes, behaviours that were fundamentally acquired from others (our parents, family and community) before we were six years old. As psychologists recognise, a majority of these developmental programmes are limiting and disempowering.

Because Switchwords talk directly to the subconscious and we work with them with an understanding of the power the subconscious has to direct our actions (and win out over our conscious mind), we can turn our subconscious into a friend rather than an enemy we must defeat. *The language of Switchwords communicates with the part of us that has most influence over our actions, decisions and attitudes.*

What the subconscious learns at night school

According to recent research at Northwestern University, Chicago, sleep could be the key to reprogramming unconscious attitudes. 'Although the tendency for people to endorse racist or sexist attitudes explicitly has decreased in recent years, social biases may nevertheless influence people's behaviour in an implicit or unconscious manner, regardless of their intentions or efforts to avoid bias,' say Gordon B. Feld and Jan Born in their report 'Unlearning implicit social biases during sleep'. In one study, the team looked at unconscious bias towards gender and race. They presented two biases: one, that science is more likely to be associated with a man than a woman; and two, that a black face is more likely to be associated with bad words than a white face.

A group of 40 white men and women were exposed to pictures of women and science-related words, such as 'maths', 'geometry' or 'physics'. Researcher Jessica Creery explains, 'We got them to strongly associate women with science words. So every time they saw a woman that was shown with a science word, they had to press a button, and every time they correctly and quickly pressed that button, they would hear a very unique sound.' (If they didn't press the button, they wouldn't hear a sound.) Then the subjects repeated the counter-bias, this time between a black face and positive words, hearing a different, distinct sound when quickly pushing the button. When the subjects were in a deep sleep, one of the sounds (for women/science or black face/good) was played to them quietly so as not to disturb them. When they woke up, the subjects were played both sounds and tested again, and the results showed they had less bias associated with the one sound they were played during sleep. This lead the researchers to deduce, in Jessica Creery's words, that 'associations that you learn while you're awake are strengthened while you're asleep'.

Although the researchers state that it's difficult to see how long the effects of the counter-bias sleep training may last – due to the reinforcement of stereotypes through the media, for example – this study does show that it is possible to reprogramme implicit social bias buried in the subconscious mind, and that sleep – an unconscious state – is the key to this learning. The report authors explain how this happens:

During sleep, information recently stored in the brain can be integrated with other information and transformed into stable representations through a process known as systems-level consolidation. The mechanisms of this transformation are thought to involve repeated reactivation of information, particularly during sleep, leading to subsequent improvement in post-sleep memory performance.

Just as sound was used as a trigger to embed a memory and strengthen an association at an unconscious level during sleep in the experiment, Switchwords, I believe, as sound vibrations that talk to the unconscious, have a similar impact, strengthening new, positive associations and reducing a bias towards unwanted beliefs. Feld and Born also suggest that 'novel sleep manipulations could be adapted to aid people in changing various unwanted or maladaptive habits, such as smoking, unhealthy eating, catastrophising or selfishness'.

To empower Switchwords by listening to them during sleep, see page 26.

Recognising self-conflict and dealing with 'block' attitudes

Blocks are logical. They have a purpose. They are not necessarily bad, limiting or disempowering. Often, they are there to protect us from a feeling associated with a memory we don't want to revisit. When blocks become not just blocks to the past but blocks to the future, however, it's time to identify why they exist and release the patterns of thinking they create. Generally, our blocks are hidden from our conscious awareness in our subconscious databank. As the subconscious drives so much of our everyday behaviour, we can often find that when we want to make positive changes to our lives we come up against conflict within. This struggle is a sign that we want to change.

Are you in conflict?

As the subconscious mind is powerful, it needs powerful motivation to change and clear old beliefs. We need to deliver this motivation in a different language, using words that don't always make sense to the conscious mind. As Colette's experience below shows (which may resonate with many of you wanting to break unhealthy habits), without the subconscious mind's agreement with your plans your efforts will be half-hearted, and being stuck in a cycle of self-conflict leads to frustration and even despair. It also means your efforts will be short-lived – after all, it's really uncomfortable to be in conflict with yourself for any length of time, so you give up on the diet, the new venture or that new job, which brings temporary relief from these feelings, but doesn't ultimately move you towards your goal.

Colette's story: Weighing up the past

Colette was 10 kilos overweight and admitted that she sabotaged her diet after around two weeks – just when she was beginning to feel and look better. She said, 'Sometimes I would really hate myself for doing it – gorging on chocolate and giving up on myself – but I would do it anyway.' Colette had been slim when a teenager and in her early twenties. She'd had a great figure ('I had a tiny waist and big boobs') and, as a consequence, lots of male interest. She dated lots of boys, and by the time she was 18 she admits she had 'a bit of a reputation. I didn't do half of the things I was accused of sexually, but somehow my body alone seemed to say it all.' When she met her long-term partner John, she piled on the weight. After her first attempt to lose weight on a sensible long-term eating plan, she organised an evening with friends at a bar. 'John was away that night and I was looking forward to going out – I'd lost loads of weight, I'd bought some new clothes, and I walked into the bar looking better than I had in years. All of a sudden, eyes were upon me. And I loved it – for the first time in ages, I was getting male attention.' But over the next three months Colette ate lots more and regained her fat.

'I came to understand that fat protected me from a part of myself I didn't trust,' she explains. 'I wanted to be with John, but being slim again took me right back to being a teenager – when I wasn't good at saying no to advances.' Colette's weight gain was logical. It served a purpose in her life, keeping away feelings of shame and guilt, but it was slowly eating away at her confidence to take control of her weight and her life.

She chanted the Switchwords FORGIVE and RESTORE. Colette is working on liking herself more and trusting that she will feel safe at whatever weight she chooses to be.

Recognising self-conflict

You know when you're in a conscious/subconscious conflict when there's negative self-talk. There's frustration, irritation and self-criticism, and projection of all this onto other people who make you feel bad because of their success. And then you're more annoyed with yourself for being negative about people you know you should applaud – and so the cycle continues. The simplest way to look at this is to honestly assess if your actions reflect your goals. Do you take action, commit to a goal and do what you say you'll do most of the time?

One key indicator of self-conflict is procrastination. When we procrastinate (becoming indecisive or reluctant to take action) it's likely that we are avoiding not just the task, but also the feelings we'll have to encounter if we do the task. If we begin that book, mow the lawn, turn down that job, will it lead to failure, regret or even a simple lack of enjoyment we don't want to deal with? Procrastination keeps us safe from feelings we don't want to feel, but procrastination also keeps us stuck. The more we procrastinate, the more the experience of procrastination itself (never mind the old experiences that might be causing it) becomes established as a neural pathway in the brain. This happens because our lived experiences cause our brain cells – neurons – to connect with each other and grow, or, as Hebb's Law has it: 'Neurons that fire together, wire together.' Procrastination becomes a habit, and the more you do it – like any habit – the more familiar it becomes. As that neural pathway grows from a country lane to a motorway, busy with avoidance thoughts, procrastination becomes the reflex response when faced with a decision. It inhibits our sense of confidence and imbues us with a lack of self-trust – we can't rely on ourselves when we need to.

 Try this: Get out of self-conflict and align with your goal

Here are two Switch-pairs to help clear the block of self-conflict: RELEASE-RESISTANCE and TOGETHER-CHANGE. First, say RELEASE-RESISTANCE. How do you feel? What's going on in your body? Did you sigh and feel a sense of release?

Now declare TOGETHER-CHANGE. TOGETHER, the master Switchword, brings your conscious and subconscious minds together as one. CHANGE clears away whatever you don't want or need (including anxiety, pain and negative thoughts – see page 65). Try also the finger-muscle test to see which Switch-pair resonates most strongly for you (see page 27).

Seeing conflict in others – Julie and Lorna

We can often recognise conflict more readily in others than in ourselves. Julie was planning her wedding. Julie had been close friends with Lorna since childhood, and they had often joked about the far-off day when one of them would get married and how they would organise each other's hen party. Lorna was single, and Julie, at 32, was getting her wedding.

Lorna was calling Julie less frequently than usual, but Lorna seemed to be saying the right thing when they did talk, albeit briefly – how happy she was for her friend, and what a lovely wedding it would be. Yet every time Julie asked Lorna for help, or even just asked her opinion on where to go for the hen party, Lorna changed the subject. The upshot was that Lorna did not do anything to arrange the party and gave a weak excuse not to attend just a few days beforehand. Lorna said one thing, yet did quite the opposite. Julie felt confused by the mixed messages.

Lorna was partly angry with Julie for getting married and abandoning her, which showed in her avoidance tactics. The other part of her that she expressed in words was the acceptable part, the part that wanted to be supportive. Lorna was in conflict with herself, unable to reconcile all her feelings about her best friend's wedding – and it showed. Julie's other friends could clearly see Lorna's dilemma; Lorna could not. She thought she had buried her feelings of jealousy, but they were there for all to see in her actions – or lack thereof.

If I had known Lorna at this time, I would have advised her to use the master Switchword TOGETHER (although she was in such denial that the problem lay with her that she may not have been open to addressing an issue she didn't perceive as hers). But when you are able to identify conflict in yourself or others, even if you don't understand the suppressed feelings behind it, you can recite or intend TOGETHER. Recite it for yourself, or project it towards the person who needs it (write their name in an Energy Circle with the word TOGETHER – see page 101).

When you declare TOGETHER, you'll find that you'll become more aware of any underlying issue that's blocking happiness or fulfilment, and be able to release it.

How Kate's Switchwords talked back

Kate didn't begin her Switchword practice with just the master Switchword TOGETHER on its own – she was keen to attract more wealth, so she began chanting the money phrase: TOGETHER-FIND-DIVINE-COUNT. She says, 'I repeated the phrase to myself often – in the mornings, when I woke up with the same old dread about being old and poor, then when walking to the train station … and whenever I could remember to do so throughout the day. I felt positive about Switchwords because I'd tried REACH in the past successfully, tracking down a book I needed for my teaching practice.

'After two weeks – and still chanting, and entering the Lottery, and checking my premium bond numbers – there was nothing. I knew I had to enter competitions and create ways for money to come to me, hence the Lottery, but I just felt I was getting nowhere. I still liked the possibility in the sound of TOGETHER-FIND-DIVINE-COUNT, though, when I recited it.

'Then came the breakthrough. I realised that as I was chanting the phrase, I was trying to visualise scratching off the third square on a scratch card to win £100,000. I could imagine scratching off one or two squares, but not the vital third. I realised then that I believed I couldn't win, or have a lot of money. Of course, I liked the idea of winning, but couldn't truthfully believe it would ever be me.'

This realisation came up during the chanting because Switchwords talk to the subconscious – Kate's subconscious had begun to talk back. And her unconscious, negative programme about money rose to the surface into her conscious awareness – into that conscious 5 per cent of our brain that has the ability to channel the 95 per cent that is usually hidden from view. This is the moment at which we make sense of a shimmery image in a bowl of water or the surface of a lake, when we look deeply into our own mirror of the self and are struck with a knowing, a self-realisation. In fairy tales, this is the moment of revelation, the culmination of all previous actions: when the Princess creeps into Bluebeard's bloody chamber to find the corpses of his former wives, or when Sleeping Beauty awakens after 100 years in a coma – a metaphor for awakening to love in the form of the Prince.

Like a Freudian slip, when a word reveals a buried belief or emotion, Kate had an 'image slip': she could not see herself – and by that I mean visualise herself – experiencing life with money. This explained some of her previous actions (and inaction) around money. Partly, she had been ambivalent. Not a materialistic person, Kate had come to have a negative attitude towards money (although she still wanted it, desperately). She never seemed to have enough money on her teacher's salary, but she comforted herself with the fact that at least she had her integrity. She wasn't corrupted by money and it wouldn't rule her life. But the longer she lived alone in the city on her pretty modest income, the harder it became to hold this attitude. Then Kate gave in to herself and decided she needed money (lots of it). Yet hiding underneath her affirmations and declarations of what she needed was the thought that 'Lots of wealthy people are sell-outs, and I'm not one of them, so I can't be wealthy.' This attitude protected her against a potential failure to achieve her goal. 'I suppose my core belief that wealth is bad, and that people who have it are bad, corrupt or somehow unworthy, was just my projection of my own feeling of unworthiness.'

By taking the action of reciting her Switchwords, Kate found a tool to uncover this negative subconscious programme. She knew now what might have been blocking her wealth: she simply didn't believe, at a deep level, that she was good enough to have it.

Expressing a block can mark the beginning of recovery. Like a computer virus infecting our subconscious databank of memories and beliefs, a block can be deleted. This may take time, but simply acknowledging that the block is there, bringing the problem to light out of shameful hiding, can be a huge step forward. Kate began to see her block just as it was: an unwanted belief, an interpretation of the past that only served to stand in the way of her having the money she needed. Why would she block herself, after all?

Dealing with shame

Shame is a powerful barrier to the truth. If an experience is accompanied by shame, it's something we often want buried. The fear of being shamed by others can be a huge motivator to cut ourselves off from the injured part that needs immediate attention and healing, pushing it as far away from our thoughts as we can in the hope that it will disappear or be forgotten. We may want to deaden the feelings of shame, as psychiatrist James Gilligan explains to Jon Ronson in Ronson's book *So You've Been Publicly Shamed*: 'Our language tells us this. One of the words we use for overwhelming shame is mortification. "I'm mortified."'

Despite our best efforts, these suppressed memories and negative experiences usually remain and at some level drive our behaviour and attitudes towards ourselves; we may suffer from lower self-esteem or self-confidence than outward appearance suggests.

 Try this: The shame soother

BOW-LOVE-RESTORE. BOW makes the feeling smaller, LOVE generates self-love and RESTORE brings confidence.

Before trying her money Switchwords again, Kate then began to choose Switchwords to help her feel more empowered, addressing her issue about not being worthy of money and what it could bring her. She chose ELATE to turn a setback to an advantage, UP for confidence and BLUFF to dispel fear, experimenting with the Switch phrases TOGETHER-UP-ELATE and TOGETHER-BLUFF.

Most of our blocks have a fear aspect, so working with Switchwords that address this can certainly help your manifesting. Switchwording brings about change, too, which can trigger fear. Losing weight, for example, means change, and many of us fear change deep down. Who would I be without my faults and problems? How would I be as a slimmer, more confident version of myself? How would other people deal with me changing? With this much going on under the surface, it's no wonder we experience fear and resistance.

Try this: The fear-busters

BLUFF helps reduce and dispel nervousness, anxiety and fear; CHANGE helps you let go of negative thoughts. Use the master Switchword TOGETHER with BLUFF and CHANGE, such as TOGETHER-BLUFF or TOGETHER-CHANGE – this gets you into a state of 'self-togetherness' when fear is making you feel separate from yourself. Add BE for peace of mind: TOGETHER-BLUFF-BE, TOGETHER-CHANGE-BE. When you begin to feel the fear ebb away, try chanting SHINE to lift your mood. You might also like to experiment with the flower-remedy Switchwords for fear (see page 108): ASPEN, CHERRY PLUM, MIMULUS, RED CHESTNUT and ROCK ROSE. Try reciting them alone, or with TOGETHER or TOGETHER-DIVINE.

A quick reminder

Know the power your subconscious has over your everyday actions. Accept that this part of you needs to be communicated with in a way that's different from conscious self-talk. Think of your subconscious as a friend who responds to authentic requests and doesn't want to be ignored, overruled or suppressed; listen to your subconscious when it 'talks back', telling you why you might be blocking your manifesting.

Three questions to ask yourself before you begin

1. What's my true goal?

Consider your goals carefully before you begin Switchwording. Do you really need money, or is it love and support? Do you really need a relationship right now, or is self-confidence more important? Be mindful of what you wish for, so that when you choose your Switchwords they express your true goal. This is not the dream come true your ego wants – it's the goal that will carry you forward through life on the right path. When your goals are authentic and you use the right Switchwords, the subconscious responds strongly and you get what you wish for. In this way, Switchwording addresses some of the 'block' issues of traditional manifesting (see the Introduction, page xv).

You may think you need money, and you chant for it (FIND-DIVINE or COUNT, for example). But during your chanting you find your mental images are more about what money can bring: freedom, choices, travel, acknowledgement, long-term security, ability to financially support others or peace of mind.

You may believe you should have a relationship, so you chant DIVINE-LOVE-CHARM-BE. You chant in the shower for a few days and find you're visualising not a romantic partner but a pet you've always wanted and have never been able to have and love.

Switchwords, therefore, can help release vital information we hold about ourselves in our subconscious. And this can be the beginning of a journey, or feedback loop, in which we can change the Switchwords we're using as we get feedback from our subconscious about what it needs. We can liken this to speed monitors on roads – they appear under speed signs saying 'Your speed is …' as you drive towards it (and your speed will usually be higher than the designated 30mph, for example). The sign gives you instant feedback and you adjust your speed accordingly. It's the same with Switchwords: when you say your words, you may find that your subconscious gives you feedback. This may come as an idea, an insight, an action you feel compelled to take, an event, a gift – and another Switchword.

 Try this: The feedback loop

Begin chanting TOGETHER, the master Switchword, for three days. Note what you feel during this time and what you receive. Sense which aspect of your life is shifting – work, relationships, money, health, home? Focus your attention here, and find a Switchword (see Chapter 3 on page 37 and the Switchword Dictionary on page 131) to support this area. If TOGETHER brings up impressions and mental images about health – for example, you're aware that your energy levels are low – try chanting MOVE for the next day or two. Again, note how you feel, and what you're feeling drawn towards. If you find after chanting TOGETHER that you're getting good feedback at work, try a work-focus Switch such as ADD to build on success. Keep the loop going, choosing a new Switchword whenever you sense a shift.

Tip: Begin with TOGETHER

If you're in doubt about which Switchwords you need now, just begin with TOGETHER and see what arises for you, or AROUND (see page 44) to help you choose from the lists in this book.

2. Can I receive what I am asking for?

Can you take a compliment without saying, 'This old thing? I've had it years …'? Can you accept a bouquet of flowers with genuine thanks rather than, 'You shouldn't have …'? Many years ago, when I travelled in Nepal, just before the end of our trip I wanted to leave some small gifts for the hotel staff. Often, travellers left unwanted clothes, shoes and money gifts – as money and clothing was hard to come by, this, we were told, would be appreciated. However, when I packaged up my items as I packed to go home, a friend living in the city where we were staying instructed us to leave the items folded on our beds. It was not done to personally place the items into the hands of the staff or to leave them at the hotel reception. The reason for this was pride. To give personally would have been seen as humiliating for the recipient. While I understood this, selfishly I wanted to give my small gifts. I wanted them to be received because I was pleased that I could leave something of some value in a place I'd so enjoyed visiting.

This got me thinking about how we receive in the West. Perhaps there's also an implied humiliation in grateful, unconditional acceptance; because we do not want to be perceived as needy, or poor, we can't say thank you without making light of the gift. However, if we cannot accept small gifts with grace, we are potentially blocking our ability to receive the greater gifts that we wish for ourselves.

These small gifts are also those little things we should appreciate more in our lives as they are, before we manifest those great desires. Showing daily gratitude for what we have activates the Law of Attraction (see page xii) – the more we recognise everyday gifts and appreciate them, the more gifts the universe sends us. Like attracts like. The more we reject our experience of the world by appearing to reject others' gifts and offers, the more our ability to manifest gets shut down.

Complaining and judging are also a form of rejection. This can occur on a subtle level. We may not perceive ourselves as moaners or critics, but think: how many times today have you complained (about the weather, your journey to work, boredom, noise ...)? Did you cast a reflex judgement on another's behaviour? That slow driver in front of you must be a **** (add – or rather, don't add – the expletive of your choice). Your words have power, and negative words create a filter through which the world appears in a darker light. My friend Kathy calls negative words 'nix-words' – or anti-Switchwords. These are the words and phrases that shut down your manifesting potential; for example, 'should', 'won't' or 'it's not ...' (Seeing or vocalising 'No', other negative words and 'fear' words such as 'poverty' and 'illness' actually cause stress-producing hormones and neurotransmitters to be released into the body.) And, as the Law of Attraction whirls into action in response to your words, negativity begets negativity. The more you put out, the more you get back.

 Try this: Gratitude practice

Every evening, make a note of what has been right about the day. Write down at least five things for which you are grateful – whether it's an easy drive to work or a novel you're enjoying, a comfortable home or being in good health that day. Even when you feel your day has been miserable, dig deep to find those five highlights. Try this for at least one week, writing your gratitude list every night. You'll find you become more able to accept the little joys of life and will more powerfully attract the greater gifts you desire. When you've finished your list, chant the Switchword THANK-YOU.

3. Can I believe and trust?

As mentioned in the Introduction (see page xv), you don't need unquestioning belief in Switchwords for them to work for you; you just need to be positive and open-minded. Some people have issues with the idea of an energetically connected, living universe or universal mind or God, which plays a part in manifesting with Switchwords, yet many people can accept, at some level, that there is a higher power at work in our lives. Choose a term or phrase you find understandable and acceptable (perhaps 'organising principle' or 'rhythm of nature'). If you cannot easily generate a belief or trust in a higher power, cultivate trust and belief in yourself to get what you need.

At the other end of the spectrum are those who are so attuned to the concept of manifesting and the Law of Attraction that they become overly attached to the outcome, constantly looking for signs that their manifesting efforts are working. When we doggedly fixate on outcomes, we are usually trapped in our ego, rather than allowing ourselves to be guided towards solutions and ideas through our intuition. Wherever you fall on the belief scale, the key issue is to summon all the belief you can when saying your Switchwords. Trust that your wish will manifest – and let go.

Completely believe in the word and your goal. Pay attention to the sensations in your body as you do this – really feel the energy of your desire. As Switchword pioneer James T. Mangan in *The Secret of Perfect Living* states:

Repeat the necessities over and over; submission to the bigger You; want, really want, your objective and state it so clearly that you can have no doubt about it. *Believe*; select the proper switch and flip it as you would an electric light switch, spending no time or thought on its meaning.

Part of the trust process is letting go of your wish and letting the result manifest.

A friend of mine, Peter, noted that when he used REACH to find a part for his bicycle, he recited the word 28 times and then waited. And guess what? Nothing happened, because he assumed it would just somehow show up – fall out of a cabinet at his feet, or that someone would find it and give it to him and there would be some huge revelation. 'Instead, I decided to recite it one more time, then forget about it for a while. I boiled the kettle, then found myself walking back to the heap of junk in a closet I'd already looked through, and I found myself sifting through some items again at the back of the closet. And it was there. I guess I was more relaxed the second time, and it appeared.'

The clue to Peter's success is in his statement 'I found myself'. He didn't will himself to do anything; he went with the flow, allowing his subconscious self to direct him.

Remember: Trust that Switchwords have a direct effect on the all-powerful subconscious and that they will bring you what you want in life.

2

Switchword Techniques
Getting started

You only have to say the word. Say your Switchword(s) aloud, intend them in your mind or repeat them so they become a mantra, again either recited aloud or silently.

Saying one word

To begin, start with one of the four manifesting Switchwords:

TOGETHER   Gets you anything you want. It magnifies the effect of any other Switchwords used with it

DIVINE   Asks for a miracle

DIVINE ORDER   Creates order at home, at work and in life

BRING   Brings you what you wish for

Combining Switchwords: Switch-pairs

To try a Switch-pair (two Switchwords used together), begin with TOGETHER-DIVINE ('manifest whatever I want and bring me a miracle'). Experiment by adding any other Switchword you choose to TOGETHER or DIVINE, or TOGETHER-DIVINE. Alternatively, choose any two Switchwords that describe your goal and chant them together; for example, LOVE-BE ('bring me love and peace').

Creating phrases

Begin with TOGETHER-DIVINE and end with BE-NOW-DONE. BE-NOW-DONE is the Switchword 'sign-off' and means, 'I make my wish with serenity and energy, and it is granted.' So to attract wealth, declare TOGETHER-DIVINE-COUNT-BE-NOW-DONE. COUNT is a Switchword for bringing in money. For love, recite TOGETHER-DIVINE-LOVE-CHARM-NOW-DONE. LOVE brings love, CHARM brings you your heart's desire. But I stress that creating phrases isn't essential; one word alone will work. Experiment with what feels right for you.

Saying and intending

First, build energy before you say the word – inject it with belief that it's going to bring you what you want. To do this, spend a few seconds or longer focusing on your goal. Feel it. Imagine you have it. If you find it difficult to summon belief, try to let go of any assumptions or biases. Have an open mind. Anything is possible – right?

Say your word or words out loud or intend them in your mind. It doesn't matter if you recite your words aloud or intend them, or alternate between the two. The words' energy and impact are the same.

Sense the sound of the words and their vibration. Feel their resonance; don't analyse the word or think about its literal meaning. Connect to its sound, its rhythm and its vibration as if you're physically absorbing it. You might imagine the word is actually a foreign word you don't understand.

If you analyse the word and think about what it means, you're engaging your conscious, analytical mind, which can lock out the intuitive subconscious. The part of you that naturally questions, analyses and judges acts as a kind of border patrol between the conscious and unconscious minds. So if you find that you are analysing or overthinking the words, give yourself a repetitive task – recite while making coffee, tidying your desk or washing up; whatever keeps your hands busy. Do this, and you'll find you encounter less interference from the conscious mind. Distract the border-control guards with an activity, and you'll get your message – your Switchword – through.

Saying Switchwords as a mantra

When you repeat a Switchword, it develops its own pulse, or rhythm, and becomes a mantra. Chanting a mantra creates a physical, emotional and mental shift. First, choose your word or phrase: for money, try COUNT, or the Switch phrase FIND-DIVINE-COUNT-ON. Repeat it – you'll instantly feel its rhythm, such as *da-dada-daaaah-da*. Your focus shifts from the words to the sound of the words, and this gets you in the vibration for success.

Try saying your words in sets of 10, 28 or 108 (the traditional mantra counts – see page xiv), allowing the words to set up their own pulse as you repeat them.

Tapping in your Switchwords

You can tap your Switchwords, too. This simple but highly effective technique, known as tapping or EFTs (Emotional Freedom Techniques), taps the words into the body's meridian points. Try rounds of tapping on the fingers and thumb, or on points on the head and torso (see Chapter 5).

Broadcasting your Switchwords through social media

Share your Switchword practice on social-media websites and Twitter – this is a great way to empower your practice. In tweets, use the hashtag Switchword, then hashtag your word or words; for example, you could tweet #Switchword #BRING as your manifesting

Switchword of the day. This not only helps Switchwording evolve through sharing, but also energises your belief in putting out what you want to the universe in the knowledge that the Law of Attraction will bring you what you want.

Embedding Switchwords during sleep

As the Northwestern University study showed (see page 5), sleep can be key to embedding change in the subconscious. Listening to your Switchwords while you sleep is an effective way to talk to your subconscious mind.

To do this, choose the Switchwords you'd like to work with – record them as a mantra (repetitions) on your phone. Play them back on a loop before you go to sleep, very quietly so you're not disturbed.

Other creative ways to work with Switchwords

Create a healing Switch-water (see Chapter 5, page 104), make Switch-cards (see below) or try your hand at Kat Miller's Energy Circles to broadcast your Switchwords (see Chapter 5, page 101).

♀ Making Switchword cards and notes

Writing your Switchwords on cards or on Post-it notes to stick to your fridge, your computer screen or the dashboard of your car not only helps you remember to say your words throughout the day, but also acts as a talisman. Write your Switchwords in the centre of the card or Post-it, then draw a complete circle around the words to enclose them (but don't let the circle touch any of the words). This turns the words into an Energy Circle (see page 101), which broadcasts them even when you're not saying them aloud or in your mind.

Testing the words that will work for you

• When you say the words, check your feelings. Saying or thinking the words creates a vibration that you may sense – this might show up as a physical sensation on your skin or elsewhere within your body, or as a feeling of lightness or a subtle shift in energy. See what resonates with you, which words you feel are right and which ones work, in that you begin to see real change in your life as a result of using them. Use your intuition to choose the words or phrases that feel best for you (use AROUND, too – see page 36). Keep a note of them in a journal – experiment with them.

• Don't worry if occasionally some Switchwords don't reso-nate for you – you may be one of the people for whom some universal Switchwords don't work (remember, univer-sal Switchwords flip switches in 95–100 per cent of people, while open Switchwords work for most people: 50–94 per cent). Try other universal or open Switchwords, or identify your personal Switchwords and find new ones that will work just for you (see Chapter 4 for ideas). Build them into your Switchword vocabulary.

Try the kinetic muscle test

An effective way to quickly test if a Switchword is right for you is to muscle-test it using your fingers. Muscle-testing works on the basis that your higher self sends a true message through the body in the form of a physical sign. It tests your energy field, like testing an electrical circuit, recognising a strong or weak connection, so it is used to generate a yes or no answer. This test is also a great technique to try out your personal Switchwords (see Chapter 4).

Before you begin, turn your attention to your body. Take a breath and let your shoulders drop. Decide to be neutral, rather than attached to any outcome. One way to do this is to focus on your solar plexus and sense your breathing so that you begin to step out of your thoughts and into your body fully. It's important to do this, because the message comes from your higher self, an aspect of your subconscious, through the sensations in your body.

- **Test the test.** Make a circle with the thumb and index finger of one hand (right or left). Now touch the tips of the index finger and thumb of the other hand together and say the word 'strong' as you firmly push them through the circle you've made with your other hand. The circle holds. This is the 'yes' position. Now repeat, saying the word 'weak'. This time, you'll find that the circle breaks; this is the 'no' position. Keep repeating this, noticing the difference between your strong and weak position. Also, pay attention to other sensations in your body – you might feel a sensation in your solar plexus, or a tingle that supports your 'yes'.
- **Say your chosen Switchword** as you push your fingers into the circle. If the circle holds, this is an affirmation that the word is appropriate for you. If it breaks, try another.
- **An alternative finger-muscle test** is to make a circle as above, but this time put the index finger of the other hand into the circle and push against the point where your fingers join. Use medium pressure and see if they separate. Again, the circle holds when you use the word 'strong', but your fingers separate and break the circle when you say 'weak'. Try this a few times and observe what happens in response to each word, then begin practising with your Switchwords.
- **Say the Switchword once only** and go with that response. If you repeat the Switchword it's likely your conscious mind

is stepping in and trying to engineer the response it wants. Stay relaxed. Do it just once and accept the answer.

Setting a time in which to receive your wish

Timing with any manifesting technique is always a complex issue. Some people believe that setting a time for their personal miracle to occur helps focus their wish, while others feel it sets up resistance, because it builds in a test – in asking for a dream to come true by precisely 10.15 a.m. tomorrow we're testing the process rather than simply believing in it. While I'm not saying it's impossible to win the Lottery tomorrow – in manifesting, *anything* is possible – a specific demand such as this could be interpreted as embedding failure before we've even begun.

Another issue is that Switchwords support states of consciousness, of being; they create conditions for success rather than offer a promise to deliver new cars or careers. You still have to do the work, earn the money, enter the Lottery and take advantage of opportunities to co-create the reality you want, but you do so with the universe and your subconscious onside.

If you'd like to try adding a time for your wishes (and I'm avoiding using the word 'limit' here, because the universe's ability to deliver what you want is limitless), add the time and date after your Switchwords. So, for example, if you want a new relationship, you could chant TOGETHER-DIVINE-LOVE-CHARM by 30 June (plus the year). Feel that you are already in your ideal relationship; chant as if you are experiencing an abundance of love, rather than a lack of it. Write down your Switchwords and the date, then forget about it. Let the universe do its work.

How do you know your Switchwords are working?

Of course, the reflex answer is, 'When I get what I want.' Yet there are ways in which you can instantly detect if a Switchword is working for you, through images, sound, feeling and validation.

Through image

Whether you say single words or recite mantras, you will find that they conjure 'flash' pictures in your mind. These images show that there's a response from the right hemisphere of your brain. The right hemisphere is responsible for face recognition, intuition, creativity and images, among many other things. It is also the subconscious part of the brain. Mental images, seen when awake or asleep, are evidence of subconscious activity. So if you find that your Switchword evokes a flash image, this as an indication that the subconscious is instantly responding to the word or phrase spoken.

This image does not need to be precise – you don't need to have glimpsed Constable's *The Hay Wain* or the contents of a bank vault when you chant one word. You may see a colour that sets a mood, or you may sense a vague shape. Some Switchworders see the word they're reciting as if written on a billboard or sign. The point is that the image is immediate – it's in your mind before you're fully aware it's there. It involves no effort and, like a dream, slips through your fingers as soon as you attempt to explain or unravel it (see also Switchwords and NLP in Chapter 6).

Through sound

When Switchwords reach into the memory of a song, it's another sign that your subconscious is responding to your words. The brain stores tunes in the subconscious, and when we hear a word it triggers a lyric and its tune, bringing it into our conscious aware-ness. If a Switchword leads you to a melody, this is a sign that again the subconscious is responding to the Switchword – it's talking back to you through music. Here's an example.

Laura's motivation star

Laura used REACH to get inspiration for her ailing project. When she said the word, she found two things happened instantly: the word conjured an image of a hand – her hand – reaching out into the sky; the word also triggered a phrase from a song – 'Reach for the stars' – and she began singing the phrase to herself. While she did this, she saw the image of her hand reaching out to touch a huge, bright yellow star. Every time she needed motivation, she chanted or sang her phrase REACH FOR THE STARS, and the image came along with it.

Through feeling

Switchwords often register in your mind and/or body as a sensa-tion. Observe what happens in your body when you choose your Switchwords (see Chapter 3) and while you're chanting them. When you first try a Switchword, be aware of any sensations in your body or impressions in your mind. Often, there's a 'flip' in the area of the stomach or heart, or an 'A-ha' – a sense of connection with a word that gives you a feeling of uplift or intrigue. (Try also the kinetic muscle test on page 27 to see which words are working for you.)

Through validation

One phenomenon that appears to happen with Switchwords is that you receive validation while you're waiting for a result, as if the universe is saying to you, 'Received and noted. Leave it with us.' Here's how Siobhan received validation that her wish for more money was being processed.

Siobhan's abundance

After her two children were born, Siobhan left an established career in marketing to be a full-time mother. She wanted to contribute to the household and attract more money into her life, but didn't know how this could happen while caring for her young children. As a member of my Switchwords email list, she received a money Switch phrase and began to use it. Siobhan says, 'I repeated the words TOGETHER-FIND-DIVINE-COUNT-ON and began deleting some tabs on my iPad when I came across Doreen Virtue's Instagram site. Right in the centre of the page was one of her affirmation cards, which read: "Your finances are improving, and there will be a positive change in your financial flow." Thinking this was a fluke, I took out of the bookcase one of her card decks, shuffled it, and guess what? I got "Blessings of Abundance".

'About two weeks later, my husband was offered regular work from a blue-chip company in the US, which was a huge relief to us. He is a freelance desktop publishing engineer and often did not know from one month to the next how much work he'd have, so it was really difficult to plan our finances. Now at least we would have regular money coming in, and at a good rate, too. Next, we managed to get a sizeable rebate on our Council Tax – our house had been incorrectly assessed since 1998! – and then I hatched an idea with a friend to begin running some paid art courses in our garden. It feels as if everything is opening up again. All hail the Switchwords!'

Frequently asked questions

Is there a particular time of day I should say my Switchwords?

You can use Switchwords any time you choose. Go for a regular time each day so you won't forget to say them, such as when you're in the shower, before you go to sleep or when you're travelling to work. It's helpful to attach your Switchword practice to a physical routine task that involves repetition – working out at the gym, or when running or walking – because it helps distract you from analysing your words, and you can add the Switchwords to the count of your physical repetitions and build up a rhythm. For example, say your words for a count of four, walk for four paces and repeat. You can make Switchwords part of your meditation practice, or your healing or creativity practice (see pages 77, 64 and 43). Many people use Switchwords to help them begin a specific task, such as meeting a deadline (DONE), beginning to write (GIGGLE) or beating procrastination whenever it strikes (MOVE).

How often should I say my Switchwords?

Say them until you get the result you need, or until you sense what's blocking you. This may be 10 minutes or several weeks. Let it become a positive habit that you build into your day.

Remember to be open to any Switchwords you're given when you begin your chanting – this is the feedback loop (see page 17), when one Switchword or phrase leads to another Switchword or phrase for you to chant.

> ## 💡 Don't wait for a problem ...
>
> Don't wait for a dilemma to hit before turning to Switchwords.
> You can use them daily to clear negative blocks to success
> (chant TOGETHER) and to attract whatever you choose,
> whether it's an old goal you've been struggling with or a
> new idea or way of living that you want to make happen.
> Switchwords boost a host of different wishes and can be used
> daily to enhance everything you do (see Chapter 3 and the
> Switchword Dictionary on page 131).

What if I want lots of things? Can I say lots of different Switchwords throughout the day?

Jo asked me if she thought she was being greedy because she could
identify so many areas of her life that needed help: more money
(lots), a relationship and new friends in an area she'd just moved to.

'Am I going to confuse myself asking for so much?' she queried.
I suggested she recite TOGETHER-DIVINE-AROUND. TOGETHER
is the master Switchword for self-alignment and manifesting (see
page 38). DIVINE asks for a miracle, which felt appropriate given
that was just how she was feeling – overwhelmed with so many
wants. AROUND would give her perspective on her situation and
help her prioritise her needs.

English isn't my first language. Are Switchwords just as effective in other languages?

The answer is yes, but we need to assume that there may be several
words that come up for one word – for example, TOGETHER could
also be interpreted as 'unity' or 'oneness'. In your own language,

choose a selection of words that have the same meaning as the Switchword in English. Say each one in turn, noting how you feel when you say it, and use the finger-muscle test (see page 27) to see if it will work for you. You may find that combining two words with a similar meaning is effective. For example, TOGETHER in German can be translated as *zusammen*, *beieinander* and *miteinander*; you may find that ZUSAMMEN works alone, or you have a stronger result in the muscle test to ZUSAMMEN-MITEINANDER. In Spanish, TOGETHER translates as *juntos* and also *unidos*; try each one individually, muscle-test them, then repeat with JUNTOS–UNIDOS to see if the combined words are more powerful for you than a single word.

Ready to begin?

To summarise, here are your simple steps to effective Switchwording:

1 Choose your goal and be ready to receive what you want (see gratitude practice on page 20).
2 Choose your Switchwords from Chapter 3 or the Switchword Dictionary (see page 131).
3 Test your Switchwords using your intuition and/or the finger-muscle test (see page 27).
4 Say, intend, chant, sing or tap them regularly, every day.
5 Believe and trust that they will work for you. Be open to how your wish might show up.
6 Note any issues that arise during your Switchwording and use the feedback loop (see page 18), adjusting your words as you go, if you need to.

If you don't see results within the time you've asked for (if you've set a time), or you otherwise feel you're not moving towards your wish, use RELEASE-RESISTANCE or chant the master Switchword TOGETHER and return to step 6.

Need motivation to get started?

Look through Chapter 3 and the Switchword Dictionary on pages
131–144 and see what appeals to you. If you're not sure whether
there's anything specific to your needs, do the following:

- Use TOGETHER to get you into alignment ready for
  choosing.
- Try AROUND first – this helps you get a better perspective.
- If you have any worry or negativity, use BLUFF to disperse
  it and get into a good frame of mind.
- Try UP for motivation ... and then begin.

3

Get What You Want

In every aspect of life

The Switchwords in this chapter are grouped by theme: Money; Work, creativity and projects; Relationships; Better health; Seven ways to use Switchwords every day. Each section lists the following category of Switchword for you to try immediately:

- **Universal Switchwords:** these work for 95–100 per cent of people
- **Open Switchwords:** these work for 50–94 per cent of people
- **Experimental Switchwords:** new Switchwords entering circulation
- **Switch-pairs:** two Switchwords used together, hyphenated
- **Switch phrases:** three or more words used together, shown hyphenated

Switch-pairs and Switch phrases combine Switchwords from any of these groups. (Please note also that the lists of Switchwords included in each section are not exhaustive – see the Switchword Dictionary, which lists 200 Switchwords, on pages 131–144, and Further Reading and Research on page 147.) Throughout this chapter are tips, techniques and case studies to demonstrate ways in which Switchwords have created change, solved problems, brought success, ideas and much more for a host of people with very different needs and wishes. Names in the case studies have been changed for reasons of confidentiality.

Experiment!

Remember, you can put together any combination of Switchwords that appeal into a Switch-pair or Switch phrase. A tried-and-tested way to begin making Switch phrases is to start your phrase with TOGETHER-DIVINE and end with BE-NOW-DONE. So to attract wealth, declare TOGETHER-DIVINE-COUNT-BE-NOW-DONE. COUNT is a Switchword for bringing in money (see below). For love, recite TOGETHER-DIVINE-LOVE-CHARM-BE-NOW-DONE. LOVE brings love, CHARM brings you heart's desire. But I stress, too, that Switch phrases are not essential; do what feels intuitively right for you. One Switchword alone is powerful. Begin with TOGETHER.

The 'master Switch': TOGETHER

TOGETHER is a 'master Switch' for everything because it creates 'self-togetherness', aligning your subconscious and conscious selves with your goals so that you can successfully attract what you want. Chanting TOGETHER also brings self-awareness, so you sense and understand any hidden blocks to manifesting what you desire.

💡 Try this: The TOGETHER mantra

Make TOGETHER a mantra by saying the word quickly, over and over (see Switchword Techniques in Chapter 2). Try this 10 times (one of the traditional mantra counts; see page xiv).

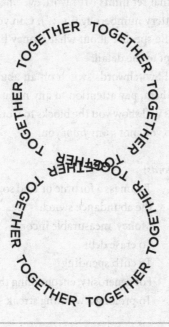

Money

Money is the flow of energy. The attitudes we hold towards money can attract it, or keep us in a state of depravation. See yourself as naturally deserving of money – without conditions. These conditions are the 'ifs' that set limits ('If I work even harder, if I'm good, if I change my Lottery numbers again …'). Can you imagine yourself with money? Be specific about what money brings you and go beyond the concept to the detail.

These financial Switchwords switch on an abundance mindset. When you chant them, pay attention to any negative thoughts that arise; Switchwords will show you the blocks to work through so that money can flow to you, not *away from* you.

Universal Switchwords:

FIND	To amass a fortune or find something of value, the abundance switch
COUNT	Money, measurable income
CANCEL	To erase debt
CUT	To curb spending
MAGNANIMITY	For generosity, encouraging the flow of money
STRETCH	To prolong a winning streak

Open Switchwords:

BINGO	To win
WINDFALL	Immediate win/payout/bonus, increase in wealth

Experimental Switchwords:

CORN	To receive abundance
CHAMPION	To find a good investment

Switch-pairs:

POVERTY-CANCEL To clear debt, to erase poverty consciousness
and help money come in

TOGETHER-SHUT To end a financial dispute

Switch phrases:

ADD-COUNT   To increase existing money

FIND-DIVINE   For a financial miracle, to find a treasure

TOGETHER-   To attract wealth as part of a team
COUNT-ON

FIND-DIVINE-   For a measurable fortune/income
COUNT-ON

See also: REACH, ON, DONE, ADJUST (pages 43 and 48)

FIND is the 'fortune' Switchword. Nadia used FIND to try to
improve her finances. FIND is the Switch for finding a fortune or
whatever is of value to you now. Nadia's email arrived just a few
hours after I'd invited her to join my Switchwords group. She'd
never heard of Switchwords, but decided to try them immediately
to improve her finances.

Nadia's little fortune

'Freakin' hell, Liz, what a system! I looked up the Switchword
for building a fortune (FIND), because I've been really, really
poor recently and needed an injection of cash almost immediately,' Nadia began. 'Anyhow, did it today while in the
shower and again just now, before checking my bank account.
Checked the account and HMRC have given me a reasonable
rebate for the taxes I just filed. It isn't a fortune yet, but it is
enough to make this month considerably easier than it was
earlier in the day when I was only expecting about a quarter
of that amount back from the taxman. Very, very grateful

and thrilled! I had been doing Huna practice in order to speak to my subconscious, but there were blocks. This feels so much more basic and straightforward. And it works! So, thanks.'

COUNT is the Switchword for finding income – counting money in. As counting is to measure, it attracts measurable income. To count is to add up, implying an increase in funds.

The Switchword author and successor to James T. Mangan Shunyam Nirav (see page 130) also suggests adding a value to COUNT in order to manifest a total. Say, think, chant or tap COUNT plus your desired figure as often as you can each day; for example, COUNT ONE HUNDRED DOLLARS – or more!

If you have felt blocked in your ability to generate money in the past, empower your Switchwords with the prefix TOGETHER-DIVINE. TOGETHER, as the master Switchword, brings your conscious and subconscious selves into alignment and switches on your manifesting power. DIVINE asks for a miracle. End your request with BE-NOW-DONE (for peace, action and the best possible delivery of your money wish).

Julia's success with FIND-DIVINE

Julia was in dire straits. She'd been waiting for two months for payment for freelance work, chasing the company who owed it, but they were still holding out. She tried COUNT and COUNT-ON but after one week was beginning to lose faith that she'd ever be paid her due. Given Julia's past experience with money – she never had enough, and this lack was becoming a consistent stress in her life – I suggested she try POVERTY-CANCEL to help clear any 'block' beliefs around money, and also to mentally direct these words to the company owing her, to release their block to paying her. She chanted POVERTY-CANCEL for a few days, until she felt a shift in attitude, then tried TOGETHER-FIND-DIVINE. The debt came in, and she smiled as she told me the amount. 'It was £440,' she said, 'and 44 is my lucky number.' For those of you who are angel-inclined, it's also the DIVINE number of the angels; when we see 44, it's a sign of guidance and protection.

CANCEL and **CUT** clear away negative beliefs or thought patterns hindering the flow of money. Use them *after* a word that describes your situation: POVERTY-CANCEL.

MAGNAMINITY Switchword originator James T. Mangan had this Switch engraved on coins for his Nation of Celestial Space (see page 127), because it keeps money circulating and inspires generosity. It means also 'to lose pettiness', and when we lose this attitude we GIVE – another Switch for generosity that also encourages selling and promotion (see page 51).

Work, creativity and projects

Need to come up with a winning strategy, solve a problem, network, take the lead, generate ideas and communicate them effectively? These Switchwords switch on innovation and maximise your potential to succeed.

Creative problem-solving

Universal Switchwords:

REACH	To solve problems, find inspiration
BRING	To manifest whatever you want or need; for motivation, creativity and success
GIGGLE	To get in the mood for writing
ON	To get ideas moving; for instant creativity
DONE	To meet a deadline
HALFWAY	To make a goal less arduous

ACT	Clear communication
AROUND	For better perspective
OPEN	To open up to inspiration

Open Switchwords:

| BREAKTHROUGH | To discover, to innovate |
| LIGHT | For inspiration and a lighter mood |

Experimental Switchwords:

| CROWN | For creative success |
| TURN | To diffuse or diminish negativity |

Switch-pairs:

| GIGGLE-DONE | To meet a writing deadline |
| HOLD-DONE | To meet a deadline while keeping the integrity of your work |

Switch phrases:

| ATTENTION-JUDGE-DONE | To complete detailed editing work |
| TOGETHER-REACH-CROWN-NOW | For creative success now |

REACH is the Switch for a creative solution. It retrieves whatever you need – from a lost object to the word or fact you can't remember – and also helps all your creative projects. If you're stuck with a blank page and can't think what to write next, REACH overcomes your block. If you're feeling under pressure and can't prioritise your work, REACH for what you need to do first to break the block. Say, think, chant, sing or tap it – and follow the next impulse you have.

Try this: Say REACH three times

Say REACH three times now. Add a rhythm or a tune behind it. What do you instantly see? Let your imagination roam for one minute. An image may arise, or a new context for REACH in a song or phrase. Write it down and sketch your image. Place this where you can see it when you need to REACH – near your keyboard, or by the bathroom mirror or fridge, for example.

Note that you're not being asked, here, to visualise anything. This would potentially corrupt the process, because you would be imposing an image upon the word – bringing in a conscious activity rather than allowing the subconscious to do its work. Laura allowed an image to arise naturally, and acknowledged the image as a way to empower her practice. When we're working with the subconscious, images surface, senses are heightened and we begin to notice more. Switchwords help us get out of the mindset that blocks creativity, because they speak directly to our subconscious and align us with our inherent power to create.

BRING it ON! Author Isaiah Hankel in his book *Black Hole Focus* reveals one powerful word he uses for motivation in his career – bring. He describes this as a meme (see page xii) rather than a Switchword, but his description echoes the impact that Switchwords have. In his role as an application scientist, he says, 'It [bring] became the answer to everyone's problems. What do we do when morale is low? Bring. What do we do if an order is messed up? Bring … People started to communicate more. Everyone's creative energy flowed.' Hankel goes on to describe how his colleagues incorporated the word into their names, embedding bring into the culture of the company: '… After a few months, everyone had a different *bring* name. There was Steve Bringfontaine, Bring Kong … and Arnold

Schwarzebringer. In my own life, I continue to use this word to keep me focused.'

An effective Switch-pair, BRING-ON is already common parlance ('bring it on') for motivation, energy and action.

GIGGLE is one of my favourites, because it gets you to write! I've shared James Mangan's gem of a Switch with many a colleague – and it really does work, particularly on those days when you need to produce (but everything else is more appealing than getting down to it). I believe the reason for the effectiveness of GIGGLE is that it reconnects us with the play aspect of creativity – which is how we learned to be creative as children. Through play, we explored and discovered the world with curiosity and wonder; by experimenting without being judged, we learned. In adult education, many a workshop begins with a play aspect, usually a basic task or game, which helps the participants connect with their play ability and bond authentically as a group. The games help us drop the roles we assume in everyday life and remember what it feels like to be childlike and free. The principle is the same: when we play, we communicate our ideas without fear of judgement – a major block to creativity.

With GIGGLE, say, think, chant or tap it, and if it's convenient, giggle to yourself– actually make yourself giggle, turning the word into an action that your subconscious recognises as a real experience. GIGGLE as you turn on your laptop or take up a pen. GIGGLE as you sketch, photograph, collect, bake or craft; GIGGLE seems to work for other pursuits as well as writing.

To make something beautiful, try CURVE. If you want to create a work of art – from an elegant interior to choosing paint colours for walls, decorating cakes, making furniture, clothes or jewellery – this one works well.

ON energises your ideas and makes them happen. ON is also the Switch for getting transport (see page 73), and in your projects it shifts them ON to the next level. Remember ON's Switchword meaning by associating it with the phrase 'Get ON with it'.

 Try this: Turn your project ON

Here's a way to use ON when you're trying to get a project off the ground: say, think, chant or tap the name of your project plus ON. Empower with the master Switch, TOGETHER, for TOGETHER-[PROJECT NAME]-ON.

DONE is the deadline Switch. Add DONE to your Switch phases to help you meet a deadline.

HALFWAY cuts down a journey time (see page 73). It helps make a deadline appear achievable – and not so far to go after all.

 Try this: Add the deadline date

You can also include the date of your deadline as follows, using its digits, so if you had a project you'd called, say, 'Project 1', which needed to be completed by 1 January 2016, you'd create this Switch phrase: TOGETHER-PROJECT-ONE-ONE-ONE-SIXTEEN-DONE.

DONE works because it puts the request in the past and implies complete trust that whatever needs to be done is instantly taken care of. At an energetic level, it is already DONE. The past-tense request resonates with other manifesting techniques because it brings the future forward, into the now, activating a time portal that opens the instant we say, think, chant or tap DONE.

Do be aware, however, that timing in any manifesting technique needs to be treated with care (see Chapter 1, page 29). Be aware of your motivation for adding any deadline to your requests – are you testing the universe, or is this really the deadline you need? The universe responds to what you need, rather than what you think you want, so be open to how any timing requests may unfold.

Tip: Add REACH

Add REACH to your Switch phrase for inspiration to get the project DONE.

Personal empowerment

Universal Switchwords:

ADJUST	To deal with problems effectively; to banish insecurity
ELATE	To turn a setback into an uplift
MONA LISA	To smile; to improve mood
DO, NOW and **HELP**	To stop procrastinating
DUCK	To not be hypersensitive
RELEASE	To exude charisma
RESTORE	To regain confidence after bullying; getting personal justice
SWING	For courage; to face a problem
UP	For confidence

Open Switchwords:

GUESS and **YES!**	To stop procrastinating
WINGS	To rise above pressure
WOLF	To make confident decisions

Experimental Switchwords:

GOLD	To thrive under pressure
HOLD	To keep your personal boundaries if feeling compromised

Switch-pairs:

TOGETHER-ADJUST	To have confidence when with a group of people; to go forward together
RESTORE-NOW	Brings you back to yourself; restores peace of mind

Switch phrases:

GUESS-NOW-BE-DONE	To stop procrastination, move forward and be at peace with your judgement

ADJUST is another word for temper, or balance, as in keeping our temper – or maintaining our equilibrium – which is exactly how we need to react when faced with pressure to make a decision or fix a problem. Say, think, chant, tap or sing ADJUST the minute a situation feels like it's running beyond your control, and do this with absolute trust that it will work.

ADJUST associates with tuning – tuning a TV channel or musical instrument so that it becomes perfectly receptive or resonant. In this way, ADJUST attunes our perspective, clearing unhelpful internal attitudes. It suggests engagement and presence; try it when you need to beat boredom. To tolerate listening to those with whom you disagree without annoyance, add CANCEL (CANCEL-ADJUST). ADJUST also helps us feel secure, so it's a great Switch to call upon when you need certainty and safe ground, mentally and emotionally.

ELATE is the power Switch – the one that turns on the juicer to make lemonade from lemons, or, as James Mangan expressed it, 'to turn a setback into an uplift'. Add ON for fast results – ELATE-ON.

MONA LISA is the smile Switch that shifts your mood upwards. Researcher Andrew Newberg comments in his book *Words Can Change Your Brain*: 'We know that smiling is a very powerful gesture; we were doing a research study looking at different symbols, and the symbol that was rated with the highest positive emotional content was the smiley face. The painting of the Mona Lisa is one particular example of that feeling of calmness.'

Say MONA LISA, and you instantly smile.

Leadership

Universal Switchwords:

TAKE	For leadership
DIVINE ORDER	To put everything in perfect order or sequence; to restore order from chaos
ACT	To be a good public speaker
ADD	To build on success
CONTINUE	To increase endurance
HORSE	To be strong; to gain power
PRAISE	To get praise from others
PUT	To build or develop

Open Switchwords:

ALL IN	Miraculous success; breakthrough

Experimental Switchwords:

CROWN   Success

TAKE flips the leadership switch, helping to bring direction and focus in groups and decision-making; it cuts through hesitation.

DIVINE ORDER puts everything in its place, as it should be; at work, it helps you see clearly what you need to do next to succeed. Switchword author Shunyam Nirav (see page 130) explains: 'Anytime you're faced with a clean-up job, or organising job of any kind, just silently repeat the Switchword DIVINE ORDER and then let yourself do whatever you get the impulse to do. It makes any task at hand as easy as is possible ...' DIVINE ORDER also works for packing for travel (see page 73), or organising your home or workplace, and can be applied to any task that involves restoring natural order, including gardening. He adds, 'If you happen to be a parent of young children, you may become very grateful for this Switchword.' In a similar vein, DIVINE ORDER also helps managers manage staff.

Sales, promotion and marketing

Universal Switchwords:

REACH   To reach out; to be creative and invent; to find inspiration; to solve problems; to find the right words

GIVE   To sell and to be generous; to be a helper

RIDICULOUS   To promote successfully; to get publicity

FOR   To promote

PERSONAL   To publish a successful website, newsletter or blog

PHASE   To set advertising or other promotional schedules

SCHEME	To design; to advertise; to produce
SHOW	To be sincere
SOPHISTICATE	To publish a successful magazine; to increase success
TINY	To be kind and courteous

Switch-pairs:

SCHEME-RIDICULOUS	To produce and sell; the entrepreneur's Switchword

Switch phrases:

TOGETHER-REACH-RIDICULOUS	To promote creatively as a team

REACH gets your message across. Have you noticed how many companies and individuals use this Switchword in their communications, as in, 'I'm reaching out to you to bring to your attention the work of ...'? When I co-edited *Kindred Spirit*, the UK's leading spiritual bi-monthly, we received hundreds of emails from US promoters using this phrase – something that didn't appear in similar missives from PRs in other countries. And we always read those REACH emails, because they seemed to lead us beyond the first two lines into a genuine request, as if they were saying, 'Let me make a real connection with you here.' REACH opened the door to us.

GIVE was the next notable Switch used in these email requests – such as, 'I'm REACHing out to you ... to GIVE you the opportunity to discover the ground-breaking work of ...' GIVE is one of the Switchwords for selling. By bringing together REACH and GIVE, these writers, perhaps without realising, called up two powerful Switchwords to get their message across. And it worked – we read and responded to more of these emails than any others. So if you're trying to promote an event, sell workshop places or are simply asking anyone for help, try REACH and GIVE in your communication with others.

RIDICULOUS is the publicity Switchword. The word 'ridiculous' comes from the Italian *ridere*, to laugh; reading or saying RIDICULOUS lightens the mood, takes away a desperation to sell and allows a playful attitude – which customers are more likely to engage with.

💡 Try this: Build relationships with TOGETHER

According to Switchword originator James T. Mangan, declaring the master Switchword TOGETHER is a brilliant way to build business relationships and also to sell. Think TOGETHER when you're with a customer, chant or tap TOGETHER before an important meeting, and use it to help you communicate and present yourself well in an interview or presentation.

How Switchwords work in marketing

Diane Boerstler, MNlp, is the founder of NLP HypnoCopy and a highly successful direct-response sales copywriter who works with business owners, coaches and entrepreneurs to build their businesses by using words that incite action to buy online.

I wrote to Diane because I noticed her using a couple of Switchwords in one of her marketing emails. As Diane is an NLP practitioner, I was aware that in NLP marketers use 'magic words' known to elicit a high response rate from customers, but the words I noticed were unusual in marketing emails: she'd included TINY and SWEET in her copy, which stood out from other 'sell' triggers we see on websites ('last chance', 'buy now', 'rich', 'instant'). Was

Diane also using Switchwords to the same effect? Here is an excerpt from an email I received from NLP HypnoCopy, with the two universal Switchwords (those that flip switches for 95–100 per cent of people) marked in bold:

Hi Liz Dean,

'I'd like to buy your ...'

'I'd like to pay you to ...'

'I'd like to hire you to ...'

'CAN YOU PLEASE SEND ME THE INVOICE ...'

(Or better yet, get them to Make You Money Now by Buying Immediately from your Website)

Imagine seeing more of these in your email ...

From your **TINY** list (as you can see I just sent it out to a **TINY** sample list of 208), see more and more and more money pouring in as your list grows bigger and bigger and bigger!

Now STOP imagining the sales you'll see, and take some action!

Be one of the first 10 people to respond with, 'Yes, Diane, please get me three times more people Joining my list, Believing what I say and Buying my products and services FAST,' and here's just a **SWEET** taste of what you'll receive ...

TINY is the Switchword for courtesy. SWEET is the Switchword for kindness.

Diane confirmed that Switchwords are intentional in her marketing copy, and that she has her own list of 'powerfully persuasive Switchwords' that trigger customers to buy a product or service. 'Because,' she explains, 'when Switchwords are read by customers, they affect the customer the same way the Switchwords affect you.' She uses Switchwords to promote her company and her clients, finding that Switchwords boost sales by up to 300 per cent.

The Magic Marketing Switchword List

Diane's list, below, blends universal Switchwords (those that flip switches in 95–100 per cent of people), open Switchwords (those that work for 50–94 per cent of people) and personal Switchwords, or those that work for an individual (see Chapter 4).

ABSOLVE	ENGAGE	QUEST
ALERT	EXCITED	REFLECT
ALONE	FILTER	RESOLVE
AMAZING	FLASH	REVEAL
ARROW	GLEAN	RUSH
BEGIN	HERO	SIMPLE
BONUS	HIDE	SNAP
BREAKTHROUGH	HIGHEST POTENTIAL	SOAR
BUFFER		SPARK
CATALYST	IMMUNITY	SUDDENLY
CHANGE	INTEND	SURRENDER
CHISEL	JACKPOT	TRANSFORM
CLEAR	KEY	TRIUMPH
CHOOSE	LIGHTNING	TRUST
CONDUIT	MARVEL	UNPLUG
CREATE	PASSION	VICTORY
CRYSTAL	PLENTY	WINDFALL
DROP	PURSUE	YES!
END	QUENCH	

Diane drafted an example of the way she weaves her magic marketing Switchwords into her copy (shown below, with Switchwords in bold); you can use this as a model for writing any type of sales copy for your product or service:

Quickly **create** a **windfall** of **plenty** straight into your **singing** bank account.

Instantly **transform** a no to a **YES!** via the **deactivation** of your prospects' subconscious mind barrier.

Naturally make your tribe **drop** their apprehensions, say, 'I'm **ALL IN**,' and **allow** them to experience an epic **breakthrough** - with you as their **compassionate conduit**.

Easily **end** the feeling that they are **alone**, and **bring** them **together** with you.

Become **crystal clear** and **alert** about why they need to **choose** what you're **offer**ing.

Allow you to **continue** to identify with their **concerns** and become the **wind** beneath their **wings**, supporting them as they **begin** turning the **wheels** of **change**.

Even **absolve** them of past mistakes so they can **begin** feeling **excited** and **engage** you as a **catalyst** for **transformation**.

💡 Try this: Write some Switchword copy

If your work involves sales and promotion, try adding Diane's Switchwords from the Magic Marketing List, and any other open or universal Switches, to your emails or advertising literature.

Finding a new job

Universal Switchwords:

COUNT	To bring measurable income
ACT	For great self-expression; to talk with confidence
AROUND	To gain perspective; to see the big picture
BLUFF	To dispel nervousness and fear
BRING	To manifest the work you want
CHARM	To bring you your heart's desire
COVER	To hide nervousness during an interview
HORSE	For strength and power
RIDICULOUS	To self-promote; to sell yourself
TINY	To be polite and courteous
TOGETHER	To build rapport during an interview
WITH	To be likeable; to get on with people

Switch-pairs:

RIDICULOUS-CHARM	To promote yourself and so get the work you most want

Switch phrases:

BRING-LIGHT-CHARM	For opportunities to find the fulfilling work you want

COUNT is one of the money Switchwords (see page 42). When you say, intend, chant or tap it, it attracts money to you by bringing ways to earn through new work opportunities.

When responding to a specific job advertisement, choose the Switchwords that best express the values that you want to communicate (select from the words above or look through the Switchword Dictionary on pages 131–144) and recite or intend them before you begin. You can also recite the words over water, sipping it while you're making your application, to keep broadcasting the words' vibrations (see page 104 for more on Switch-water). If teamwork is a key aspect of the role, try WITH for cooperation and likeability; if leadership is a criterion, intend HORSE to communicate power and strength. AROUND broadcasts your ability to see an organisation at a group level and says that you're a strategist.

💡 Try this: Switch up your job application

Writing or intending Switchwords on any materials connected with your application helps empower your request for fulfilling work and bring the work to you. Before you email a CV or response letter to a job advertisement or make an approach to a new client, on your screen use your finger to trace a Switchword or phrase: try RIDICULOUS-CHARM, for example, to promote yourself and ensure your application is seen and read; CHARM brings you the work you desire.

Education, research and tests

Here are the power-words you'll need to get into the study zone: they will help you improve your concentration, 'save' key facts as you go, hit a deadline and ultimately get through that work without distraction.

Universal Switchwords:

NEXT	To get through lots of detailed, repetitive work
ATTENTION	To pay attention to detail; to avoid carelessness
CARE	To remember; to retain information
DONE	To easily meet a deadline
HALFWAY	To make your goal feel achievable

JUDGE	To get into the mood for reading and studying
PHASE	To set a revision schedule
REACH	To retrieve information
WATCH	To learn a new skill or technique

Open Switchwords:

BINGO	To get the right answer; to make the right move (also helps when playing games, quizzes)
GUESS	To stop procrastinating and avoiding work

Experimental Switchwords:

PASS	To pass an examination; to remain calm
STICK	To hold attention; to concentrate

Switch-pairs:

CARE-REACH	To learn and recall at will
RESTORE-CARE	To improve memory
GIGGLE-DONE	To meet a writing deadline

Switch phrases:

ATTENTION-NEXT-DONE	To work with accuracy and to deadline

CARE is the 'revision' Switch. According to Switchword author Shunyam Nirav (see page 130), 'What you care about, you remember; if you don't care, you won't remember.' He likens CARE to the SAVE command function: say it when you come across a significant fact or statement you want to remember. Likewise, it's also a helpful Switchword for remembering people's names – silently repeat the name in your mind, then add CARE: JOHN DOE-CARE.

> ## 💡 Tip: Use REACH to retrieve information
>
> As CARE stores, REACH retrieves. Chant REACH when you need instant recall.

NEXT gets you through detailed work that's a bore or a burden. Try NEXT when you're absorbed with revision or other study, fact-checking or editing, when you're working through budgets or when you have that onerous tax return to submit.

PASS is an experimental Switchword that has had success bringing calm in the face of exam adversity.

Julie's PASS

Julie didn't intend to find a Switchword for her pre-exam panic, but this personal Switch came to her one evening when she was feeling frustrated and particularly nervous. She saw herself taking the exam – walking into the exam room, looking at the question paper and beginning to write – then heard the word PASS. 'I just kept hearing it in my head, so I started to say it in my mind. It wasn't just because I wanted to pass – the word seemed to keep me calm and less panicky whenever I had a rush of fear about the exam day. I chanted it like a mantra before the exam, intended it in my mind when I got stuck on a question – and after the exam, when the results came in, I did pass.'

Relationships: romance and friendships

We have multiple potential soulmates and true friends; the trick is to recognise them when they appear in our lives. Switchwords help shift your vibration at a deeper level of the subconscious, so you attract the people who are right for you now and, in existing partnerships, strengthen your bond. When you declare, chant, sing or tap your words, you may like to visualise a pink, glowing light around you that expands as you repeat your words.

Attracting a new relationship

Universal Switchwords:

CHARM	To get your heart's desire
BRING	To attract and manifest love
GIVE	To be emotionally available
SWEET	To make a good impression
HOLE	To be attractive; to have charisma
PRAISE	To make yourself beautiful or handsome
CHUCKLE	To show your personality

Open Switchwords:

LOVE	To generate and attract love
SHINE	To attract special attention and dispel negativity

Switch phrases:

BRING-ON-LOVE-DIVINE	For a love miracle; bring me my soulmate

CHARM is the 'heart's desire' Switch; it works when you focus on a goal that is your genuine wish, from a new relationship to a child (see page 73). When your wish is authentic and comes from a place of love rather than need, CHARM creates the opportunities for your wish to be delivered.

 Try this: The Switch mantra to attract a new relationship

Chant this phrase 10 times and repeat morning and evening, and when you can throughout the day:

'Thank you for bringing me my perfect love. BRING-ON-LOVE-DIVINE.'

The first statement assumes trust that the universe will deliver your request; the Switch phrase asks for a love miracle now.

Dealing with relationship issues

Universal Switchwords:

TOGETHER	The master Switchword; gets you anything you want. It magnifies the effect of any other Switchwords used with it
SLOW	To have patience
POSTPONE	To stop sulking
CONCEDE	To stop quarrelling
CUT	To avoid saying something you'll regret
REJOICE	To not be jealous
REVERSE	To bury a grudge; to forgive
PRAISE	To stop finding fault

Open Switchwords:

LOVE	To generate and attract love
MUSIC	To connect in love and harmony
FORGIVE	To forgive; to end resentment or the need for revenge

Experimental Switchwords:

LENNON   To reconcile; to find love and peace

Switch-pairs:

CONCEDE-   For forgiveness; to clear lingering negative
CLEAR   issues

Switch phrases:

BOW-   To let go of past hurts
CONCEDE-FORGIVE

TOGETHER, the master Switchword, improves all relationships in life: business relationships, romantic partnerships and friendships.

> ### 💡 Try this: Reconnect with TOGETHER
>
> When you and your partner chant TOGETHER simultaneously, you reconnect with your whole self and strengthen the bond between you. TOGETHER helps eliminate the feeling of being disconnected, and allows any issues that need attention to arise. Add ACT, chanting the Switch phrase TOGETHER-ACT, to improve communication.

REVERSE creates forgiveness. Do you need to end a war, forgive or let go of the past in some way? Before you try it, consider if you can and do forgive. Even when you cannot comprehend the motives of the person who crossed you, there's still a case for forgiveness (for your sake) so that you can stop expending energy ruminating on the past. So, forgive for your benefit, say REVERSE and let go. To forgive yourself for past actions, say, think or chant REVERSE-ME.

Exes, enemies and frenemies: What to do about negative people in your life

To stop thinking about a person and/or distance yourself from them or the effect of their actions, say the person's full name plus CUT. If a relationship or friendship is broken and it is time to move on, mentally send them a love bomb by chanting the Switch phrase DIVINE-THANKS for the role they played in your life but which is now over. TOGETHER-ADJUST-TINY-THANKS switches the charge of your energy away from irritation, anger and frustration – which keep you connected – to acceptance, which releases you both.

Better health

Switchwords can help manage symptoms of physical illness, but they are by no means a cure. If an ailment is caused by underlying beliefs, memories and attitudes, Switchwords can have a positive effect, just like other energy-healing techniques such as EFTs.

Managing pain

Universal Switchwords:

ALONE	To heal
CHANGE	To create an energy-shift, easing emotional and physical pain (also to get something out of the eye)
CANCEL	To get rid of whatever you don't want: negative thoughts, pain or discomfort
BE	Good health; a return to good form
MOVE	For energy
SWING	For courage to confront a situation

Open Switchwords:

WINGS   To rise above pain; to move freely

Switch-pairs:

CHANGE-BE   To shift or soothe pain through acceptance of it
TOGETHER-   To see underlying reasons for physical pain; to
CHANGE   release fear

Switch phrases:

ALONE-   To heal physically, mentally and/or spiritually;
DIVINE-MOVE   to give energy

(See also the flower-remedy Switchwords for personality traits on pages 107–113.)

ALONE is the Switch for healing; in *The Secret of Perfect Living*, James T. Mangan's definition is 'to heal a scab'. Later experiments with this word show it helps healing in general, and improves our ability to care for and nurture ourselves.

CHANGE helps switch off pain. Try chanting CHANGE whenever pain recurs, with the awareness that Switchwords may help you manage (but not cure) pain associated with long-term conditions, while helping to relieve the temporary pain associated with a headache or other physical discomfort.

When working with Switchwords, it is important that we genuinely want to let go of our pain. This may seem obvious, but sometimes physical ailments stay with us because they have a deeper significance. Recurrent pain can be a symptom of unresolved emotion, such as anger, guilt or fear – particularly of change. The issues underlying pain may also serve a purpose. Author and medical intuitive Caroline Myss calls this 'woundology' – when a person seeks continual acknowledgement of their condition to manipulate others' reactions rather than fully heal. When we are ready to let go not just of the pain but of any underlying reasons for the pain, CHANGE can work for you. If you feel you might be resisting change, add the master Switchword TOGETHER and think, say or tap TOGETHER-CHANGE.

As with all Switchword practice, you need to believe it works – with experience, you will come to believe this, but to clear any negative assumptions before you try CHANGE or TOGETHER-CHANGE, start with TOGETHER-CLEAR. This cleans up your beliefs and shifts any negative thinking patterns. It's also a great Switch to use for anxiety and depression. You can use BLUFF for negativity, too.

CANCEL it! CANCEL is another powerful Switch to help with physical symptoms. Here's how Joan, 71, worked with a CANCEL Switch-phrase, which had a remarkable impact on the frequency and intensity of her migraine attacks.

Managing migraines

Joan had suffered from severe migraines since her mid-forties. A bad week was characterised by three or more migraines with an aura, affecting her balance and sight, which drove her to bed for hours. No matter how many changes she made to her diet, the type of medication she took or the doctors she saw, nothing touched the relentless pain she felt. Joan was beginning to feel she was losing her battle with her pain, and that her migraines would limit her everyday life for the future. She no longer went shopping or travelled alone.

I asked her to experiment with CANCEL and prefix it with a word that described her experience of the migraine pain – she could be very specific (we discussed RED HOT NEEDLES and FLASH CUT). However, after some consideration, she said she wanted to try PAIN and see how she got on. Every morning, Joan recited PAIN-CANCEL in her mind while she drank her first cup of tea in bed. When she had low energy during the day (Joan also has fibromyalgia, a chronic pain condition) she repeated PAIN-CANCEL. On day three, she fully expected a migraine to come. It didn't. Encouraged, her belief in her Switch-phrase grew and she kept repeating PAIN-CANCEL. She also tried a little tapping, saying the phrase aloud as she tapped on each finger (see Chapter 6). In all, Jean had nine days without a migraine.

Her migraines haven't disappeared completely, but now they hit her less frequently. And when they do come, she feels more confident about managing the pain with PAIN-CANCEL. Joan now takes fewer painkillers, so she suffers fewer side-effects of the medication.

Emotions: Low mood and anxiety

Universal Switchwords:

BLUFF	To reduce anxiety
CLEAR/CANCEL	To banish negative thoughts
BE	For peace of mind and good health

Experimental Switchwords:

SHINE	To lift a mood; clear negativity; to bless

Switch-pairs:

PURGE-CANCEL/ **POSTPONE-** **CANCEL**	To banish negative thoughts and behaviours

Switch phrases:

PURGE-CANCEL- **DONE**	To instantly protect yourself from other people's negative emotions

(See also the emotional-healing flower-remedy Switches on pages 107–113.)

BLUFF is a great soother, helping to dispel nervousness. It appears to work well even with long-term anxiety, as this case study reveals.

Judith's BLUFF

When working with Judith, a recent client who had suffered anxiety all her life, she confessed that she felt as if her anxious feelings had become hard-wired into her brain, as if her anxiety had become a part of her personality. She began to speak about the issues that worried her, over which she had no control: an ageing relative she cared for, potential redundancy, her husband's health issues, her son's unemployment ... the list went on. The multiple foci of her anxieties cycled on from one day to the next. When I suggested she chant BLUFF to clear anxiety, as she repeated the word I got the image of an eraser rubbing out black anxiety over her torso area and turning it white. 'Is it BLUFF because BLUFF is like fluff – a bit of nothing?' she asked, before answering her own question: 'I think it is. That's what it feels like. Fluff that just floats away.' Judith and I had different reactions to the word, in that she saw the reason BLUFF might work for her, whereas I saw how the result might look – as if all her anxieties were erased in an instant. 'For some reason, I just feel lighter now,' Judith continued. 'As if my anxiety has suddenly lifted.' And this happened without lots of chanting; just repeating the word once began a process that was to see Judith in the coming weeks begin to step out of a thought-habit that she feared would imprison her for life.

Sarah's anti-anxiety Switch

With a history of reactive anxiety and depression, Sarah didn't want to turn to antidepressants again when she suffered a second miscarriage. She experimented with tapping (see Chapter 6) and Switchwords together, using the universal Switch CLEAR, which began to bring some relief from her symptoms. Next, she experimented with the Switch-pair PURGE-CANCEL, which she found had a more powerful effect, and as she gradually began to experience better moods, she took advantage of these good times with the universal Switch STRETCH – to make a positive experience last longer. Using PURGE-CANCEL and STRETCH as and when she needed them, Sarah began to manage her symptoms, and suffered fewer episodes of anxiety.

 Tip: CANCEL whatever is holding you back

You can apply CANCEL to any attitudes or beliefs that may be holding you back, such as poverty consciousness, or combine CANCEL with the name of a person you're having unwanted negative thoughts about (see Relationships, page 61). Negative thoughts drain our energy. CANCEL them and you'll feel more positive, relaxed and in control.

SHINE helps delete negativity and lifts your mood; it also helps clear you of others' negative energy and comments. This is a great Switch to use at the beginning of the day if you suffer from low mood on waking, or whenever you need to lift your spirits – and then feel the sunshine return!

Try this: Say, think, chant or sing the SHINE mantra

Repeat TOGETHER, TOGETHER, TOGETHER! SHINE, SHINE, SHINE or SHINE-ON, 28 times.

Jo's SHINE

I'd given Jo (who works as a homeopath) this new Switchword mantra to try, and it showed up some notable results. 'I chanted SHINE, SHINE, SHINE between clients to shift the energy in my consulting room and stop me feeling so drained. It certainly worked, but after a few days I began to sense it was affecting me in a way I hadn't expected. I began to notice all sorts of irritations – casual negative comments, the low mood in a friend's home after she'd had her mother to stay, the traffic … How could SHINE be doing this? On reflection, though, I realised that perhaps SHINE was having a cleansing effect on me, too, and that the negatives were arising so I could see for the first time the impact these negatives were having upon me. Maybe my vibration was rising, and because of that shift the negatives were becoming more noticeable. I felt able to observe this, without becoming so affected by it.'

Weight loss and addiction issues

Universal Switchwords:

OFF	To quit a bad habit
CUT	To control excess and improve self-care
OFFER	To not be greedy
PRAISE	To like your body
BE	For good health
COUNT	To cut down on smoking
RESTORE	To restore what you feel you have lost (for example, the figure/health you once had)
SAVE	To stop drinking

Switch-pairs:

PURGE-CANCEL	To get rid of thoughts that sabotage well-being

RESTORE-BE   To be the person you were before the addiction; to return to good health

Switch phrases:
TOGETHER-   To be committed to healthy weight loss
OFFER-BE

OFF is the 'quit' Switch that helps you quit thinking when you need to sleep (see page 78), and motivates you to quit habits that no longer serve you. It can be particularly effective when used in tapping (see Chapter 6), and when combined with TOGETHER, as this empowers the command to quit: TOGETHER-OFF.

CUT is the Switchword for curbing your excesses – the word to use when you're sorely tempted to eat or drink more than usual.

Use CUT to help you eat and drink more mindfully – that is, with conscious awareness of what you're consuming. Without this awareness, the cake/brandy/second hot chocolate will have hit your lips before you have a chance to interject with CUT.

Eating mindfully is, first of all, to consider what you're going to eat before you eat it. This planning stage is our point of power and choice. If you're browsing a menu, think CUT to help you make a balanced choice, whether this is choosing mainly healthy foods and one treat, or letting yourself off the strict diet for a night. CUT guides you subconsciously to do what is best for you, and you only – regardless of what other people are eating.

OFFER helps you moderate your portions while you eat. Think OFFER when you first begin to feel full to prevent overeating.

John's diet solution

John's struggle with weight loss mirrors many a diet story. Stuck for years in a cycle of on-off dieting, he would lose a few kilos, put them all back on, then start a new diet – with the same effect. Some of his diets lasted a few days, others a few months. But the long-term result was always the same: he returned to his pre-diet shape, usually around 10 kilos over the ideal weight for his height and age.

John used CUT when he was food shopping to make sure he didn't buy too many sweet treats, and also while he was cooking, so as not to make too many tempting leftovers. At around 9 p.m. when he got the nibbles, he'd chant it again.

It worked for the first few weeks, but the effect of his Switchword didn't last.

He tried again. He thought about his beliefs about his diet. He'd been dieting so long that he'd forgotten why he was really doing it. To get into 34-inch-waist trousers? To not feel so flabby or unfit? Or just because he'd got into repeating this ongoing battle within himself?

To deal with the build-up of his need to comfort-eat at night, he chose the Switch-pair PURGE-CANCEL to help get rid of the thoughts that were driving his actions. He wrote it on a large Post-it note, which he stuck to the front of the fridge door. Whenever he wanted to open the fridge for a snack, he read the note, chanted CUT again and found he could walk away from the fridge most times – enough to have a positive impact on his waistline.

> ### 💡 Tip: More ways to benefit from the power of CUT
>
> Use CUT, too, when you need to control spending and protect your over-maxed credit card. CUT also curbs your tongue when you're about to say something you'll later regret.

Pregnancy and fertility

BRING is a manifesting Switchword, helping you create whatever you want – and it's a powerful activator for pregnancy. Combine it with CHARM, which brings you your heart's desire, and COPY, which resonates with increased fertility. If getting pregnant feels like you're asking for a miracle, prefix this with DIVINE, the 'miracle-maker' word. NOW adds speed. Say, think, chant or sing the Switch phrase: DIVINE-CHARM-BRING-COPY-NOW.

Seven ways to use Switchwords every day

1. Travelling

Universal Switchwords:

ON	To get a journey going; to hail a cab, catch a bus, get a lift
GUARD	To protect personal space or property
HALFWAY	Reduces your experience of a journey time by half
DIVINE ORDER	To get organised; to pack before a journey

ON is the 'green-light' Switch, helping you get where you're going. Try it next time you need a cab or when you want any other type of transport to show up. ON also energises other Switchwords, because it imparts ambition and productivity; it makes your projects happen. Try adding it to NEXT to speed up arduous detailed work: NEXT-ON. Or use TURN-ON to turn away from negatives and get a surge of positive energy and ideas.

2. To find lost objects and fire up your memory

Universal Switchword:

REACH   To find a lost object; to solve problems

REACH, the 'lightbulb' Switchword for solving problems and finding inspiration (see page 44), is one of the most frequently used, because it also brings back lost objects. We all seem capable of losing small items at least once a day (glasses, car keys, a book, paperwork ...) and REACH is the perfect response. You can also declare REACH to retrieve information you know but can't recall – names, facts, places. And as the anecdote below shows, REACH can also help retrieve larger items from a distance.

How REACH returned a car

'I must tell you what happened two weeks ago ...' Kim wrote to me. 'In January my son and his girlfriend moved to a beautiful flat and purchased their first brand-new car together. I thought at last they were settled and that things were looking great. Then on 10 March they got broken into and the spare car key was stolen and they [the thieves] stole the car. The police said if they did not find it after two-to-three days they must write it off. As you can imagine, it was devastating; the three days passed, and nothing. So I decided to do the REACH Switchword. I imagined the car like a dinky toy and when I said the word REACH I visualised picking the car up and putting it back on their drive. Lo and behold, seven days later the car was found abandoned without a scratch on it and the key in the ignition! Forensics took the car for prints, but the car is now back safe and sound. I could not believe it! This is really powerful stuff.'

3. For an energy boost

Universal Switchwords:

NOW	To follow a good impulse; to get active
BUBBLE	For energy and excitement
CRISP	To rejuvenate; to feel energised
UP	For instant confidence

Open Switchwords:

WOLF	For stamina and confidence
YES!	For motivation

Experimental Switchword:

SHINE	To instantly lift the mood

Switch-pair:

NOW-DONE	For a fast result; can be added after other Switchwords (see page 24)

NOW makes it happen NOW. It ends procrastination, bringing energy and motivation. Complete a Switch-phrase with NOW or NOW-DONE as a 'sign-off' to deliver your wish with extra speed.

4. For instant wisdom

Universal Switchwords:

AROUND   For a wider perspective

SLOW   For patience and wisdom

Open Switchwords:

OWL   For a new angle on a situation

WINGS   To rise above it all; to see the bigger picture

Switch-pairs:

SLOW-LOVE   To act from a place of love rather than fear

SLOW creates the mental space to make wise choices. When we SLOW down, we notice more, observing more acutely others' input, the environment we're in and our own internal processes. Chant SLOW to activate your inner wisdom before making a decision.

5. For everything to run smoothly throughout the day

Universal Switchwords:

DIVINE ORDER To be organised and efficient; to create harmony

ELATE   To turn a setback to your advantage

BOW   To make a problem smaller

DIVINE ORDER helps you get everything done efficiently at work and at home. Chant it, then follow the impulse you next have to organise, plan, arrange and tidy up. This is a brilliant Switchword to call upon when you feel overwhelmed and need to multitask but don't know where to begin. Rather than writing a strict to-do list and following it to the letter, start with DIVINE ORDER and you will see that what needs to be done gets done, in just the right way.

♡ Try this: DIVINE ORDER plus HALFWAY

DIVINE ORDER plus HALFWAY helps speed up a tidying, organising or 'sorting' task. Jen, for example, needed to make 30 sets of earrings for a jewellery fair, but to begin she had to take a bag of over 100 mixed beads and separate them according to their colour and type. She chanted DIVINE ORDER-HALFWAY as she sorted the beads and found that she completed the sorting more quickly than usual – and that it didn't feel so arduous.

6. To de-stress

Universal Switchwords:
HO   To sigh; to relax

Experimental Switchword:
ROOM   To have personal space; to wind down

Switch-pairs:
ROOM-ME   For 'me' time; to have privacy
BEACH-ME   To unwind; to stretch out

HO is the Switchword used to induce a sigh, and to let go and relax. I find this works best when vocalised rather than intended in the mind, so whisper or say HO aloud. Try it now – it's almost impossible to say without sighing – letting your shoulders drop and becoming instantly more relaxed. It's a great way, too, to prepare for meditation and sleep, particularly if you're stressed or overthinking.

7. To get to sleep

Universal Switchword:
OFF   To get to sleep

Open Switchword:
LAVENDER   To relax and sleep

Experimental Switchwords:
STOP   To stop overthinking; to promote sleep
OCEAN   To dream

Switch-pair:
CRYSTAL-   For lucid dreaming
OCEAN

OFF is the 'off switch' that gets you to sleep, switching OFF the thoughts that keep you awake.

 Try this: OFF to sleep in one breath

Inhale deeply, and as you exhale, count '5, 4, 3, 2, 1, OFF'. Repeat as you drift off to sleep; this generally takes around four or five repetitions.

4

Finding Your Personal Switchwords

Unique words for you

Personal Switchwords are the power-words that work just for you. They may be words with a family connection, lyrics from a song or favourite words that for some reason just feel right. These are not the 'catchphrases' we absorb socially that drift in and out of fashion (remember 'game on'?), but words that act as a direct, personal link to a positive feeling or memory. Jackie loves the word 'scenery' because it reminds her of the wonderful views in the North Yorkshire Dales; it gives her a feeling of freshness and perspective. Jayne loves 'rose' because she connects it with opportunities coming her way – like a rose opening up. Yasia loves 'bumblebee' because her daughter's middle name is Bee.

Other favourites arise because there's a quality about the word itself that attracts us, such as the rhythm or vowel sound – feel the pulse when you say 'pumpernickel', the sigh when you say 'moon' or the way your tongue moves with 'sglodion', Tracey's beloved Welsh word for chips.

Whichever words attract you, take note. You can dedicate them as Switchwords and combine them to create powerful phrases. For example, Jayne's is TOGETHER-ROSE-BE-DONE-NOW ('make me one in my purpose, bring abundance right away').

Three techniques to find your personal Switchwords

The techniques below will help you detect your personal Switchwords, from looking around your home for clues to a short meditation to allow you to sense the words that work for you.

1. Detect your favourite words

A London literature festival asked people to vote for their favourite English word. From the 15,000 people who responded came this top 10:

1 Serendipity
2 Quidditch
3 Love
4 Peace/Why
5 Onomatopoeia (a word that describes the sound it makes, such as 'bang')
6 Hope
7 Faith
8 Football/Muggle/Hello/Family
9 Compassion/Home
10 Jesus/Money

Which are your favourite words? The words you love may be more obvious than you think. Note the artwork you have around you and words they include, look at greetings cards you keep forever, wall art (the words LOVE and PEACE in sculpted letters are popular), even tattoos. Write down your favourites, then use the finger-muscle test on page 27 to test their strength for you as new personal Switchwords.

2. Ask for your Switchwords with visualisation

This visualisation is a gentle way to allow subconscious images to arise. The names of these images, colours or shapes can become your personal Switchwords. To prepare, find a quiet space in which to sit comfortably, and have a pen and paper at the ready.

1 Sit quietly for a moment. Take a deep breath, and breathe out. Imagine you are following the path of your breath through your body with your mind's eye. Feel your body softening as you relax. Close your eyes.

2 Chant the master Switchword TOGETHER 10 times. Sit in silence for a few moments.

3 Visualise a screen floating before you, right in your line of sight. It is white and glowing. Ask, 'What do I need?'

4 Sense any colours, objects or impressions that emerge on the screen and be aware of any word that snaps into your mind. Write down this word.

5 Close your eyes again, take a deep breath in and out, then focus on this word. Ask, 'What does this [your word] do for me?' When you sense the answer to this question, you've made the link between the word and its effect. Write it down. Open your eyes, and come back to the room.

6 Use the finger-muscle test (see page 27) to see how strongly you respond to your new word. Dedicate this word as a personal Switch. Chant TOGETHER plus your word(s) as many times as you like and pay attention to the feeling you get when you do this. For example, say you saw orange on your screen and sensed the word FIRE. You would then ask, 'What does FIRE do for me?' Anya got FIRE and felt a flip in her solar plexus when she asked that question; she began to feel strong and

focused. She used FIRE as her personal Switch to help her concentrate and succeed when she was running – 'firing on all cylinders'.

In the days after this exercise, do not be surprised if you see your word when you're not actively looking for it – on a magazine cover, a billboard, on an internet pop-up ad, on the side of a truck. 'As soon as I'd found my personal Switch, it was as if it was being broadcast everywhere,' says Alain. And it wasn't a common word, like 'now' or 'win': 'My word was FLOW. The morning after that word came to me, I glimpsed a magazine cover in a newsagent at the station with the headline "Go with the flow", then later that day a DVD with the title *Flow Yoga* on a colleague's desk. On the way home that night, my partner picked me up from the station – on the radio was the Bellamy Brothers' tune "Let Your Love Flow". It just kept coming.'

3. Say one, find another

Here's how. Say you choose a Switchword to help deal with pain – CHANGE (CHANGE helps diminish or delete whatever you don't want in your life, from pain to difficult relationships, habits and obsessing). You chant it as often as you want to, usually as often as you remember to throughout the day. As you chant, or after you've finished, another word comes to mind. It may not be on the Switchword lists in this book, but it feels important to you. (Let's say that word is HONEY. It feels kind of soothing.) So you begin to chant it, and it feels right, so you add it to CHANGE, chanting CHANGE-HONEY, or use HONEY on its own. You experiment with both, and find that you're less aware of your pain when you chant your new word on its own. Congratulations – you've just discovered a new personal Switchword! By talking to your subconscious with the first word, CHANGE, you've flipped a switch – and as a result you have accessed another power-word to work with. This may also happen to you when trying the feed-back loop, beginning with the master Switch TOGETHER (see page 18).

Christopher's TURN lightened the load

Christopher discovered a personal switch, TURN, also by beginning with CHANGE. He suffers from a chronic pain condition, fibromyalgia, although his concern was not the ongoing pain, but dealing with the negative thoughts that flooded through him just after he woke up every morning. 'I think it's because I've had so many years of dealing with this condition, it's just wearing me down,' he explained. He often spent the first two hours or so of each morning just trying to 'will' himself into a better frame of mind. 'But talking to myself like this just made me more aware of how bad I was really feeling,' he continued. 'So I tried a self-help CD, which gave me some visualisations to try, which did improve things a bit.' One of the visualisations involved putting unwanted feelings into a 'swirl' and swirling them so fast they disappeared. 'When I tried this, I saw a word in my mind – TURN. It led me to see the swirl as a washing machine. After I learned about Switchwords, I decided to work more on the washing-machine image. I put all the negative words I was feeling – sadness, frustration, irritation, hopelessness – into the washing machine. Then I saw myself putting the Switchword CHANGE in, too – like adding washing powder. Then to switch on the cycle, I chanted TURN. And I'd see the washing machine spinning away all the negative words. Afterwards, I always feel brighter.'

Choosing real names as Switchwords

Names can become dedicated as Switchwords because names have immediate resonance. Celebrities often change their names to become famous. Marketing companies use algorithms to personalise mass emails with the name of the recipient. See your name, and it's impossible not to pay attention. Your name can become a personal Switchword, because you respond more to your own name than virtually any other word or phrase.

The magic of the name is reinforced by our oldest stories and fables – discovering a person's true name is a bargaining tool for power. Rumpelstiltskin challenges a queen to guess his true name or give him her first-born child. When she discovers the name, Rumpelstiltskin tears himself in two, never to return. In Egyptian mythology, Isis, the goddess of magic, tricks the creator-god Ra into revealing his true name, which was written on his heart and known to no man. In return, she gains the power of life and death. Even within the story, the true name of Ra is not revealed.

Real names in Switchword practice are largely culturally defined. The name of the American actor CHARLTON HESTON has become a Switchword to stand tall, while martial arts instructor and film legend BRUCE LEE imparts strength and energy. Although Switchwords work on vibration (see the Introduction), when choosing real names as Switches it's more about the association you have with that person rather than the poetics of sound. MONA LISA has been adopted as a Switchword for smiling (and when you say MONA LISA, it's impossible not to smile, because we instantly think of the famous smile in that painting); it works because Leonardo da Vinci's *Mona Lisa* is a universal icon.

💡 Try this: Go for a hero

Choose your personal heroes and use their names as Switchwords to attract their attributes of success into your life. This may be from any discipline you like – sports, music, a spiritual guru, peacemaker, scientist or actor. They may also be people you know whom you love and respect. Trudy picked the name of her dog, Samuel, because she gets an intense loving feeling whenever she chants SAMUEL as a Switchword. When she wants to be more compassionate to people who irritate her, she mentally intends SAMUEL.

Try out the feel of the name first, and pay attention to what sensations arise with the word. Be sure that the feeling is positive. If any thoughts of frustration or envy arise ('Why can't I be like him/her?'), choose another hero name – one that engenders positives such as hope, affection and inspiration.

Personal numbers: Switchword enhancers

Numbers, just like words, have energy – each digit holds a vibration. A number that resonates for you can be added to a Switchword to create word pairs or phrases to enhance your practice.

Your lucky number

Dedicating your lucky number as a Switchword is a great way to boost your manifesting, summoning all the help of the universe for money luck or to help you on the day of an interview, presentation, examination or other test. Take your lucky number and add the master Switch TOGETHER – for example, TOGETHER-SEVEN if your lucky number is seven (TOGETHER brings self-togetherness, aligning you for luck). To ask for a miracle and to further empower your request, add DIVINE, giving the personal Switch phrase TOGETHER-DIVINE-SEVEN.

Aligning with your purpose: your life-path number

Your life-path number is your date of birth reduced to numbers 1–9, 11 or 22, which are the key numbers in numerology. If you were born on 20 October 1976 this would be: 20 + 10 (for the 10th month) + 1 + 9 + 7 + 6, which gives 53; 5 + 3 equals a life-path number of EIGHT. If your date of birth doesn't initially add up to one of these numbers (if it comes out at 10 or 12 for example), keep adding the digits until you end up with either 1–9, 11 or 22. Add the number to TOGETHER (plus any more Switchwords of your choice) to create a powerful Switch phrase that helps you sense your life direction.

Which number vibration do you need now?

Rather than working solely from your life-path or lucky number, you can also take a look at the number meanings below and intuitively choose one that represents the energy you need at a specific moment or on a particular day. If you have more than one issue, take both numbers together. For example, if you wanted to have confidence to speak up and lead and also want stability in your home life, you would choose numbers 1 and 4 from the list below and create a Switch phrase like TOGETHER-DIVINE-ONE-FOUR. It's advisable to choose a maximum of two numbers, otherwise you dilute the request. Remember, if you have a multitude of needs, reciting TOGETHER can be enough, and trust that whatever is most important for you to have will come to you first. Let the universe decide what it is you genuinely need.

Life-path number meanings

ONE: Self-esteem; individuality; singular purpose; leadership; energy

TWO: Partnership or wanting commitment; the need for agreement while respecting others' views and requirements

THREE: Creativity; time for play and developing skills, taking time out; taking calculated risks; getting pregnant

FOUR: Pythagoras' number for justice, based on good proportion; fairness; stability; financial improvement; a reality check; to focus on getting the basics right; planning

FIVE: Choices and commitment

SIX: Harmony; flow; nostalgia

SEVEN: The pursuit of knowledge, discovery and travel; to recognise the potential in you and in others

EIGHT: Enjoying the journey rather than the destination; balancing work and play

NINE: Results; reward; satisfaction; intensity; taking an overview; looking to the future; learning from the past

ELEVEN: Great potential achievement; intuition, connection to the unconscious; faith, clairvoyance

TWENTY-TWO: Great success as a result of grounded, practical ambition

5

Switchword Healing

Reiki, Energy Circles and healing frequency numbers

Switchwords have a place in the healing of the self and others. As Switchwording is a form of manifesting through energy alignment, it can be an effective addition to healing modalities, which work on the same basis: a healing practitioner develops sensitivity to energetic imbalances within the body, and redresses them via direct or indirect touch through the energy body, or aura, that surrounds the physical body. In some schools of reiki, for example, symbols are visualised on the body during the healing session. Words are compacted symbols; chant them and they decompress, transmitting an energy form – a symbol, in other words. For this reason, Switchwords can be powerful tools in your healing practice, and can also benefit those of you who are not practitioners but would like to work on personal self-healing.

Switchwording in healing is in its infancy. Many of the Switchwords suggested here are experimental. As we delve more deeply into Switchword healing in the future, there may be many more Switches to flip to assist healing and personal growth. Do remember, however, that the original manifesting Switchwords – TOGETHER, DIVINE, BRING and REACH – can be used very effectively for healing, too. Because TOGETHER brings our subconscious and conscious into alignment, it helps negate inner conflict, which can be the cause of dis-ease. Add them to your Switch phrases or Switch-pairs to empower your Switchword mantras.

ANGEL-LIGHT-DIVINE-BE	The angelic blessing; to call upon the angels for help; to ask for healing
ELOHIM-DIVINE	To ask God/the universe for a miracle
I AM-DIVINE-BE	I honour my divinity/spirituality
I AM	To connect with the higher self – the authentic self, or who we really are
PURE-LIGHT-BE	To cleanse a space and purify the environment
ENVELOPE or WRAP	For spiritual protection
DATA-DIVINE-OPEN	To access the akashic records
DIVINE LIGHT	To connect with the source
SHINE	To raise the vibration; to bless (see page 69)
ANGEL-LIGHT-DIVINE-	To bless, to make anything better; for divine help in removing obstacles

ANGEL-LIGHT-DIVINE-BE is the angelic blessing. It invites healing, miracles, guidance, love and peace. You can chant this for self-healing, and also to send healing to others from a distance.

Self-healing: Place your hands over your heart chakra or the part of the body where you feel discomfort or pain. Take a deep breath and on the outbreak chant or intend ANGEL-LIGHT-DIVINE-BE. Let your breathing return to normal for a minute or two and really sense you are within your heart, your emotions and within your body; register all the subtle sensations you feel in your limbs, neck, torso, feet and hands. Sense any change in temperature, and any shift in pain or feeling. Then repeat the deep breath and chant once or twice more.

Distant healing: Visualise the person in a bubble of pink light. Mentally project the words ANGEL-LIGHT-DIVINE-BE within the bubble, over the person's image. Connect this image with your heart chakra, as if there's an invisible cord linking you to the pink bubble. Visualise that you're sending energy down the cord and into the bubble so that the pink of the bubble and the Switchwords ANGEL-LIGHT-DIVINE-BE become more vivid and alive. Feel that your energy is broadcasting the Switchwords to the person in the bubble, and out to the universe.

ANGEL-LIGHT-DIVINE-BE also appears to help animals, as Alison's experience suggests.

How Alison helped her dog heal

Alison's whippet lurcher, Purdy, was recently diagnosed with cancer in her leg. Alison was devastated at this news from their vet, who gave her two choices: to put her to sleep or to remove the diseased limb. Alison, of course, saw no option but to go ahead with the amputation, which she knew would leave Purdy traumatised. For several weeks before the operation, Alison stroked Purdy, looked into her eyes and softly chanted the Switch phrase ANGEL-LIGHT-DIVINE-BE. After the operation, the vet was amazed by how well Purdy had coped with the surgery – and how fast she was recovering. Alison continues to chant her calming Switchwords to Purdy as she returns to full strength.

> 💡 **Try this: Experiment with the healing Switchwords**
>
> Which healing Switchwords resonate for you? Experiment with combinations of words, tuning into their vibration as you think, say, chant or sing them (and muscle-test, too, to see which are strongest for you – see page 27). Sound healer Petra Galligan combined TOGETHER, DIVINE and SHINE to create her mantra 'TOGETHER, TOGETHER, TOGETHER, SHINE, SHINE, SHINE, DIVINE' to prepare herself for healing and for connection to her higher self throughout the day. She explains: 'I sing it first thing in the morning in an ascending melody, three times, and it really hits the spot. The repetition of three seems to connect immediately to the angelic realms and Christ consciousness, and adding DIVINE creates a guided-missile effect straight to the soul or higher self. It's been working a treat for me and I seem to have a much clearer connection now with spiritual guidance and my higher self.'
>
> Also, try visualisation to get your personal Switchwords (see Chapter 4).

Chakra Switchwords

According to Sanskrit literature, each of the seven principal chakras, or bio-energy points on the body, has an associated bija mantra (*bija* is a one-syllable sound, or seed). When the mantra is intoned with particular attention to the placement of the tongue and lips, the subtle energy channels of the body are purified. The mantra sound may also have been designed to hit a sequence of meridian points inside the mouth. Dr David Shannahoff-Khalsa, a researcher in mind-body dynamics at the University of California, suggests that mantra repetition enables the tongue to stimulate the acupuncture meridians, particularly on the roof of the mouth. This stimulation causes chemical changes in the brain.

The mantra invites physical, emotional and spiritual healing, and higher levels of spiritual awareness. From the root or base chakra to the crown, the bija mantra for each is pronounced 'lang' (base), 'vang' (sacral), 'rang' (solar plexus), 'yang' (heart), 'hang' (throat), 'aum' (third eye) and 'aum' (also for the crown chakra). Sound is a healer; as bodies of energy, we are affected by the vibration of a word, even when we do not know its meaning.

While the origins of chakra attunement through sound are ancient – chanting bija mantra for the five elements, which connect to the chakras, was first documented in the Jabala Darsana Upanishad (200 BCE – 200 CE) – the Switchwords below for chakra healing attunement and alignment are new, evolving through my practice and that of other practitioners in my field (see the Acknowledgements on page 155) who generously shared their experiences of self- and client-healing.

DIVINE-LIGHT-ADJUST	To harmonise the chakras
DIVINE ORDER	For chakra alignment
PURE or CLEAR	To remove energetic blocks in chakras
SHAKTI-DIVINE-FLOWER or OPEN-ME	To open the chakras
SHAKTI-FOREVER	To close the chakras
SHAKTI-PURE-CRYSTAL-HALFWAY	To keep the crown and third-eye chakras partially open

Switchwords for attuning the seven principal chakras

Chakra	Switchword	Location
Root or base chakra	HOME	Genitals
Sacral chakra	SWEET	An inch below the navel
Solar plexus chakra	JEWEL	At the solar plexus
Heart chakra	LOVE	At the heart
Throat chakra	I AM	At the throat, around the Adam's apple
Third-eye chakra	CRYSTAL	Between the eyebrows
Crown chakra	PURE	The crown of the head

You can also experiment with Switchwords that link with a chakra's associations. For example, the base chakra is linked with the need for grounding and security, and relates to financial stability. Try a finance Switch when working on this chakra by adding one or more of the finance words to the chakra attunement word.

For example, for the root or base chakra HOME, add FIND or COUNT, so chant or intend HOME-FIND or HOME-COUNT or HOME-FIND-COUNT while working on this chakra point during a healing session. For self-healing, place your hand on your root or base chakra (at the base of the spine or at the position of the genitals) and chant or intend. For the sacral chakra, try JEWEL-UP; for the solar plexus, PEACE-MOVE; for the heart, LOVE-CHARM; for the throat, I AM-FOR-GIVE; for the third-eye or brow chakra, try CRYSTAL-BETWEEN, and for the crown chakra, try PURE-CRYSTAL. It's important to experiment with which words resonate for you, as the practitioner, and which intuitively feel right for the client. You may equally find that one Switchword is perfect for attuning all the chakras. UP is a great Switch for energising, so you may feel comfortable applying this one Switchword to each chakra point. Also experiment with PURE, for removing chakra blocks, and Julie Leivers' Switchword HUM, for chakra alignment (see below).

Chakra	Association	Switchwords to boost
Root or base chakra	Money, security, groundedness	FIND, COUNT
Sacral chakra	Sexuality, creativity, fertility, identity	HOLD, ON, REACH, UP
Solar plexus chakra	Energy, empowerment, emotions (fear, excitement)	MOVE, SWING
Heart chakra	Love	LOVE, CHARM, CURVE
Throat chakra	Communication, truth	FOR, GIVE
Third eye chakra	Intuition, insight	BETWEEN, CRYSTAL
Crown chakra	Purity, spiritual connection, consciousness, unity	OPEN, CRYSTAL

🔆 Try this: HUM at the end

Reiki master Julie Leivers, when experimenting with chakra Switchwords, tried her Switchword HUM towards the end of a reiki treatment on a client. She says, 'In order for all the chakras to synchronise vibration, I hovered my hand towards the patient's head and stretched out my arms towards the root chakra, as far as I could without discomfort, and chanted the word HUM – and it was quite powerful. I will certainly use this again in my sessions.' Her client told her she, too, had felt the vibration of HUM.

Switch phrases for chakra issues

Root chakra issues
Feeling insecure, vulnerable, poor
Chant: PURE-DIVINE-ORDER-COUNT

Sacral chakra issues
Creative block, fertility issues, feeling your boundaries are compromised
Chant: SWEET-DIVINE-ORDER-HOLD

Solar plexus chakra issues
Low energy levels, lack of motivation, fear, physical ailments
Chant: JEWEL-DIVINE-ORDER-MOVE

Heart chakra issues
Heartbreak, loss, betrayal, sadness, lack of self-compassion
Chant: LOVE-DIVINE-ORDER-CHARM

Throat chakra issues
Poor self-expression, repressed feelings, inability to be in your truth
Chant: I-AM-DIVINE-ORDER-FOR

Third-eye chakra issues
Mistrust in your own intuition, blocking out feelings
Chant: CRYSTAL-DIVINE-ORDER-BETWEEN

Crown chakra issues
Feeling disconnected with the self and the outside word; aloneness
Chant: PURE-DIVINE-ORDER-OPEN

💡 Try this: A Switchword healing ritual

Here's how you might flow through a healing treatment using Switchwords. It's suggested that these words are used in addition to your usual practice.

To cleanse a space: PURE-SHINE-LIGHT-BE

To prepare to give healing: TOGETHER-DIVINE

To protect yourself spiritually during the healing: ENVELOPE, and intend ENVELOPE to protect the recipient

To ground yourself: ROOT

To open the chakras: OPEN-ME or SHAKTI-DIVINE-FLOWER

To raise your vibration: SHINE

To call in guides/angels/masters: ANGEL-LIGHT-DIVINE-SHINE

During the healing session: Choose the chakra words (see page 94), or simply chant DIVINE ORDER.

Use HUM to feel the vibration of all the chakras in alignment (see page 97).

To close down the chakras after a healing session: SHAKTI-FOREVER

To give gratitude: THANKS-BE-DONE

You might recommend Switchwords from this book to help your clients, such as AROUND to get a better sense of perspective or to make decisions, CHANGE to help manage pain or unwanted thoughts or UP for confidence. Again, teaching the master Switch TOGETHER is a great starting point before progressing to Switch-pairs and phrases.

To access the akashic records

To access: DATA-OPEN-DIVINE-SOURCE plus your name

To clear down your akashic record of negative karmic inheritance: CHARGE-CLEAR

The akashic record is a databank of the experience of our past incarnations – a library of our soul's journeys. When we access the akasha, usually through meditation and prayer, we sense our karmic inheritance. While in our akashic records, we can clear unwanted negative karma inherited from past lives. Chant or mentally intend CLEAR-CHARGE to affect this process.

Switchwords for intuitive readings

CRYSTAL	For clairvoyance
BETWEEN	For intuition and psychic ability
LISTEN	To see the future
REACH	For psychometry (to read an object)

Meditation to channel the Switchwords you need

1　Find a comfortable, quiet space. Sit with the soles of your feet on the floor and your hands loosely by your side.

2　Take a deep breath in through your nose and out through your mouth. Visualise that you're exhaling anything you don't need (what you should be doing, to-do lists, etc.) and inhaling pure white light that fills your body. While you begin to feel lighter inside, feel the weight of your body in your chair. Tune in to how your body is feeling. Take two more breaths like this, then let your natural breathing pattern return.

3　Chant TOGETHER-BETWEEN as a mantra – so the words take on a rhythm – eight or 28 times. TOGETHER, the master Switchword, brings you into subconscious-conscious alignment, so you're ready to make a request to the universe; BETWEEN activates intuition.

4　Ask the universe/your spiritual guides to show you a word that's right for you. It might come as a sound, a picture or a scent or colour.

Switchword Energy Circles

An Energy Circle is an energy-activation tool used for distant healing. Originated by Kat Miller (see the box, below), Energy Circles broadcast to a person, a place or a situation; they can contain Switchwords, flower-remedy names, healing frequency numbers (see the lists on pages 107 and 114) and other healing therapy names of your choice. You can also create an Energy Circle just for you, by writing your name in the circle. Here are Kat's methods and tips:

1　Take a piece of paper. Write the recipient of your Switch-words, such as your name, the name of another person, the name of a place or the situation.

2 Under this, write the Switchwords you want to send – you can also include flower-remedy names (see page 107) and healing frequency numbers (see page 114).

3 Take your pen or any writing implement (highlighter pen, pencil, crayon, coloured pencil or paint – whatever you choose) and draw a complete, unbroken circle, encompassing all the words. The two end lines of the circle must meet or cross over each other if the circle is to work. The line of the circle should not touch any of the words within the circle.

4 If you are creating an Energy Circle for yourself, you can write things you do not want in your experience – but these must be written outside the circle, not within it.

5 Activate the circle by placing it on a flat surface or pinning it to a wall. It's still active if you can't see it, so it's fine if it's kept flat in a folder or notebook – just keep it face up. An Energy Circle is temporarily deactivated when it is face down.

MILLIE
LOVE 528
ROCK ROSE

MILLIE is the focus of the healing; LOVE increases love; 528 is the Solfeggio number that brings love and miracles; ROCK ROSE is the flower-remedy name that switches from fear into serenity.

Tip: Try other shapes

You can use any unbroken shape rather than a circle. For example, for love, you might draw a heart and enclose your name and Switchwords within it; for money, you might use the oblong shape of a dollar bill or euro note. Choose any shape you like, provided it has one continuous line and is closed. Kat Miller's research on Energy Circles also suggests that corners tend to trap energy, so if you're making a heart or a rectangle, square or diamond, draw rounded rather than sharp corners.

How to permanently close an energy circle

Fold the paper so that any part of the circle is folded, or crumple the paper or throw it in the bin.

The origins of Energy Circles

Energy circles were originated by Kat Miller, founder of the Blue Iris Learning Center, which holds the largest Switchword database in the world (see Further Reading and Research on page 147 for website details). Kat explains how Switchword Energy Circles began when a friend told her that she was 'broadcasting' Bach Rescue Remedy to another person by adding the remedy drops to a glass of water, setting the glass on a circle drawn on paper, with an arrow pointing to another circle with that person's name in it – effectively, a form of distant healing (healing directed at a person not physically present). Kat developed this technique by writing the person's name inside a circle and setting the water on it (rather than having a second circle with an arrow) and, as she says, 'Energy Circles were born.'

Kat and her friend then discovered that Switchwords, numbers, homeopathic remedy names and more could be written into Energy Circles, then the person's name was added to it, and whatever was included in the circle would be effectively broadcast directly to that person for healing. 'We also found that Energy Circles including names should generally be limited to three per person, as more seem to either overwhelm or randomly deactivate one or more [of the circles],' Kat explains. 'However, we have found no limit to the number of Energy Circles that can be set up.'

Attuning water with Switchwords and flower-remedy names

Water holds and magnifies the vibration of Switchwords. Research by Dr Masaru Emoto in Japan suggests water, when subjected to particular thoughts, forms particular ice crystals: the vibration of thought affects the way the crystals form. From his research, which began in 1994, he observed how distilled water exposed to positive influences – music, prayer, pictures and letters – produced the most beautiful, unique crystals when frozen, compared to distilled water exposed to opposite, negative inputs, which produced deformed, unique crystals on freezing. He explains: 'Everything is a combination of energetic vibration. As vibration resonates, it makes some tangible objects.' By exposing Switchwords to water, the water becomes a medium for the transfer of the vibration of our Switches, inviting 'tangible objects' – or results. Like flower remedies (see below), which carry the signature vibration or life energy of a plant bathed in water over a period of time, Switch-water carries the code, the vibrational essence of the Switchword, which empowers your ability to manifest.

> ### ♀ Try this: Making a Switch-water
>
> Fill a glass or a bottle with water. Hold it and either say or intend your Switchwords over the water for a few minutes, repeating them as a mantra (you can repeat your words 10, 28 or 108 times). Drink a little of the water. The Switchwords will continue to empower the water when you are not drinking it, so you can continue to sip it throughout the day.

> ### ♀ Tip: Write the words on the container
>
> You can also write your Switchwords on your water bottle before you chant. Write them with any suitable implement on the bottle. If you're using a glass, write your Switchwords with your finger; there doesn't need to be mist or condensation on the glass for the words to show up. Simply trace out the words on the glass as a symbol of your intention.

Kat's happy water

Kat Miller, who discovered Energy Circles and the application of Energy Circles to water, experimented with Switch-water – what she calls 'Happy Water' – and discovered that tasting the water before and after writing Switchwords on the vessel usually shows a change in the flavour of the water. She explains: 'My sister has a reverse-osmosis water filter at home [a water purifier]. She lives about a half-hour away from the big city. Whenever she came down to the big city, she would bring a cooler full of bottles of RO water with her. She always drank only her own water.

'One day she was visiting me. I wanted to show her what I had discovered about writing LOVE on the water vessels. I took some tap water (unfiltered) and asked her to please taste it. Her reaction was very hesitant and she said "blech" when she did taste a tiny bit of it. She said it smelled and tasted like bleach.

'I then had her write LOVE on the vessel with her finger and taste it. She was amazed that it tasted good, and within a few minutes she'd drunk the whole cup of water. The bleach had completely dissipated. She no longer carries RO water with her wherever she goes, she just turns her water into Happy Water and enjoys it.'

💡 Try this: Place your Switch-water on an Energy Circle

'We found that it takes approximately 15 seconds to charge water with the contents of an Energy Circle,' Kat Miller explains, 'and that one can sequentially charge water with multiple Energy Circles, then drink the water.'

1   Create your Energy Circle(s) as described on pages 101–102, beginning with the name of the person, place or situation (or your name), and adding your chosen Switchwords and flower-remedy Switchwords, then enclosing all the words in a drawn, unbroken circle.

2   Place a bottle or glass of water on the Energy Circle, and after 15 seconds the water is charged and ready to drink.

The Switchwords stay in the water even when it is removed from the Energy Circle, and it's also fine to leave the water on the Energy Circle for an indefinite period of time.

Flower-remedy Switchwords for emotional healing

Flower remedies are natural medicine for the emotions and the soul, helping to correct energy imbalances that cause behavioural patterns. Flower-remedy names have become adopted as healing Switchwords. You can also add these words to your Energy Circles.

Oversensitivity

AGRIMONY

Personality traits: Wearing a mask – a smile that hides anxiety; those who fear conflict and sacrifice their feelings as a result
Switchword: Helps with self-expression, feeling at peace

CENTAURY

Personality traits: The inability to say no; martyrdom; the need to serve and please others to excess
Switchword: Gives inner strength

HOLLY

Personality traits/situation: Unreasonable jealousy, envy, revenge, suspicion
Switchword: Helps open the heart to divine love

WALNUT

Personality trait/situation: Being occasionally led astray by others
Switchword: Brings protection from outside influences

Fear

ASPEN

Personality trait/condition: Vague, unknown fears; nightmares
Switchword: Eases anxiety

CHERRY PLUM

Personality traits/situation: Irrational fears, potential nervous breakdown
Switchword: Helps to restore balance and control over the mind

MIMULUS

Personality trait/situation: Fear of particular situations such as poverty or loneliness, which they keep quiet about
Switchword: Brings courage

RED CHESTNUT

Personality trait/situation: Fear about loved ones, anxiety for their well-being, anticipating misfortune
Switchword: Brings trust that they will be looked after by the universe

ROCK ROSE

Situation: Panic, extreme fear
Switchword: Helps to restore calm

Overcare and concern

BEECH

Personality traits: Intolerance, inflexible attitudes, criticism of others
Switchword: Helps to see the good things in life

CHICORY

Personality trait: Suffocating love, overprotectiveness, possessive love
Switchword: Helps to restore self-love and unconditional love for others

ROCK WATER

Personality traits/situation: Martyrdom, suppressing one's own needs, self-denial
Switchword: Helps to restore a flexible attitude

VERVAIN

Personality traits/situation: Overenthusiasm, overwork, perfectionism, fixed ideas
Switchword: Restores balance

VINE

Personality traits/situation: Dominance, bullying, confidence, arrogance
Switchword: Balances the heart and mind

Uncertainty

CERATO

Personality traits/situation: Lack of trust in inner guidance/intuition; lack of confidence, listening too much to others
Switchword: Gives a sense of certainty and self-trust

GORSE

Personality traits/situation: Hopelessness and despair, can be experienced by those who are ill
Switchword: Brings hope and vision

GENTIAN

Personality traits/situation: Doubt, loss of faith, feeling disconnected from source, being disheartened by a setback
Switchword: Helps restore trust

HORNBEAM

Personality traits/situation: Procrastination, no mental energy, feeling tired at the thought of doing anything
Switchword: Helps to bring motivation

MUSTARD

Personality trait/situation: Random black moods resulting in withdrawal from others
Switchword: Brings back happiness

OLIVE

Personality traits/situation: Burn-out, complete exhaustion after mental or physical work, finding no pleasure in life
Switchword: Brings energy

SCLERANTHUS

Personality traits/situation: Indecisiveness, swinging from one position to another, not usually sharing this with others
Switchword: Brings balance

WILD OAT

Personality traits/situation: Searching for a sense of purpose, the need to know which career to follow
Switchword: Brings certainty

Lack of interest, apathy

CHESTNUT BUD

Personality trait: Not learning from repeated mistakes or unhelpful behaviour patterns

Switchword: Helps one move on by learning the lessons of the past

CLEMATIS

Personality traits/situation: Dreaminess, lack of concentration, ungroundedness, living in the future

Switchword: Brings a reality check, and the ability to be fully present

HONEYSUCKLE

Personality traits/situation: Living in the past, inability to deal with change or loss

Switchword: Helps with living in the present and accepting the way things are

WHITE CHESTNUT

Personality traits/situation: Unwanted recurring thoughts, mental clutter

Switchword: Brings peace

WILD ROSE

Personality traits: Surrender, apathy, lack of motivation; tiredness and boredom

Switchword: Brings enthusiasm

CRAB APPLE

Personality trait/situation: Feeling unworthy or unclean

Switchword: Helps release the belief or emotional memory

ELM
Personality trait/situation: Feeling overwhelmed and despondent due to too much responsibility
Switchword: Restores the ability to cope and care for the self in a balanced way

Loneliness

HEATHER
Personality trait/situation: Cannot bear to be alone, compulsive talking
Switchword: Encourages listening and sharing, and less self-centredness

IMPATIENS
Personality trait: Impatience, interrupting others when they speak, wanting to do things on their own
Switchword: Helps to bring balance and feel less driven

WATER VIOLET
Personality trait: Extreme self-reliance; quiet type with a tendency to withdraw into themselves and appear aloof
Switchword: Brings the ability to communicate with others

Despondency and despair

LARCH
Personality trait/situation: Not being good enough, feeling inferior
Switchword: Brings self-confidence

OAK
Personality trait: The determined struggler, ever-hopeful in the face of ongoing challenges
Switchword: Brings strength

PINE

Personality trait/situation: Guilt and self-blame even when not at fault
Switchword: Brings self-worth

STAR OF BETHLEHEM

Situation: Shock, loss, trauma
Switchword: Helps recovery, eases emotional numbing

SWEET CHESTNUT

Personality trait/situation: Desolation; the dark night of the soul –
reaching the limit before a personal breakthrough
Switchword: Brings hope and joy

WILLOW

Personality trait/situation: Victimhood and resentment
Switchword: Brings forgiveness

Choosing a flower-remedy Switchword

Look at the list above and get a feel for which words you are attracted
to. Then use the finger-muscle test (see page 27) to find which
words you resonate with – say the word as you try to break a finger-
and-thumb circle with the finger of your opposite hand. If the circle
holds, it affirms the word for you; if it breaks when you declare
the word, this is a weak word for you with lower resonance. Take
the flower-remedy names that affirm for you, and put them with
any Switchwords that support your aim. For example, to recover
from shock or injury, try STAR OF BETHLEHEM-BE (STAR OF
BETHLEHEM helps trauma; BE brings peace). For anxiety, try
BLUFF-ASPEN (BLUFF and ASPEN both help anxiety). You can
say the Switchwords in the order that feels right to you. Also, you
can include a flower-remedy Switchword in your Energy Circles
(see page 101).

Put in the Hertz: wavelength frequency numbers

Wavelength frequency numbers, usually expressed in Hertz (Hz), or cycles per second, may be used with your Switchwords to empower or specify a request. They are often added to Energy Circles (see page 101).

The sources of these numbers are incredibly diverse, from brainwave frequencies to the 'lost' musical scale known as Solfeggio. Then there are the Schumann resonances, predictors of lightning, and the Rife Scale, a range of healing frequencies based on the controversial practice of radionics. There's no unifying system; healing numbers, used as an adjunct to our usual Switchwords, appear to be a collection gleaned from varying traditions, proposed as thought-medicine for ailments or triggers for changes in consciousness. For your reference, here are just a few examples taken from the hundreds of healing numbers that may be combined with Switchwords:

- **Brainwave frequency numbers:** 10Hz is associated with the release of serotonin – to improve mood and concentration. This is a brainwave frequency, an alpha state at which the brain exhibits relaxed optimism. The 'peak performance' brainwave frequency is 40Hz (some sources also claim this is possible at 10Hz). For 'peak performance' during, say, a sporting event, you might choose TOGETHER-FIGHT-40. TOGETHER, the master Switch, aligns your subconscious and conscious beliefs; FIGHT is to win in a competition; 40 supports peak performance in that competition.

- **The Schumann resonances numbers:** 7.83Hz is perhaps regarded as the heartbeat frequency of the planet, as it is necessary for our physical functioning; spacecrafts have generators to mimic this frequency to ensure the well-being of the astronauts. Winfried Otto Schumann (1888–1974), a German physicist, calculated the Schumann resonances, which are a series of low-frequency peaks in the earth's electromagnetic field caused by lightning. Although there is no significant data that currently links these precise frequencies with states of mind, the resonances, listed below, have come to have associations with mental functioning:

7.83Hz: the fundamental resonance, the pulse of earth

14.3Hz: stimulating, helps studying

20.8Hz: improves brain function, energising

27.3Hz (an octave above 7.83Hz) and 33.8Hz: creative thinking, concentration

- **Solfeggio Scale numbers:** If you've heard of 528Hz as the 'love' frequency, here is why. The Solfeggio is a six-note scale used in Gregorian chant. In order to get the monks to sing the scale in tune, Guido of Arezzo (c. 991–1033) taught the eighth-century hymn *'Ut Queant Laxis'* ('Hymn to St John the Baptist') to his choirs because it included all six notes in ascending phrases.

C *'Ut quenat laxis'* – 'do let our voices'*
396Hz: liberating guilt and fear

D *'Resonare fibris'* – 'resonate purely'
417Hz: undoing situations and making change

E *'Mira gestorum'* – 'miracles telling'
528Hz: love, transformation and miracles; the repair frequency for damaged DNA

F *'Famuli tuorum'* – 'far greater than many'
639Hz: reconnection, finding balance and understanding relationships

G *'Solve polluti'* – 'so let our tongues be'
741Hz: solving problems, self-expression

A *'Labi reatum, Sancte Iohannes'* – 'lavish in your praises, Saint John the Baptist'
852Hz: awakening intuition, spiritual order
(*Paraphrased translations by Cecile Gertkenn, 1902–2001.)

There are also secondary tones available in the Solfeggio Scale:

963Hz: to awaken a state of perfection
174Hz: to reduce pain

We can see the relationship between note E, 528Hz, and miracles; *'mira gestorum'* translates as 'miracles telling' or 'wonders of your deeds'. *'Solve pollute'*, 'so let our tongues be', implies the interpretation 'solving problems, self-expression'.

The frequencies associated with each note were suggested by Dr Joseph Puleo and Leonard G. Horowitz, but given that the hymn was composed in the eighth century, before concert tuning, we cannot with absolute certainty know that note E, for example, would have vibrated at 528 cycles per second. Number theorists suggest that the pattern of numbers that make up the Solfeggio frequencies – 1, 7, 4, 2, 8, 5 and 3, 9, 6 – may relate to mathematical or mystical number systems. As with all Switchwords, explore which work for you. You can listen to 528Hz frequencies, and the other Solfeggio frequencies, on many websites, and also try out their viability with the finger-muscle test (see page 27).

- **The Rife Scale frequencies:** American inventor Royal Raymond Rife (1888–1971) developed a machine that emitted resonances believed to destroy or weaken disease-inducing pathogens, such as bacteria, to counteract disease in the body. For example, 10,000Hz is the Rife Scale frequency for treating alcoholism, abdominal pain, earaches and head-aches, among other ailments. Rife's findings and his machine were rejected by the medical community, because they could not be independently verified. However, interest in his work continues; see http://www.rife.de for further information.

Creating a healing-number Switch phrase: Solfeggio numbers

DIVINE ORDER-396
DIVINE ORDER-417
DIVINE ORDER-528
DIVINE ORDER-639
DIVINE ORDER-741
DIVINE ORDER-852

Or combine the numbers with which you resonate with Switch-words that bring you your goal. For example:

For love, try LOVE-528 (Solfeggio)
For creative writing, try GIGGLE-ON-27.3 (Schumann)

Using healing numbers in Energy Circles

You can also add healing numbers to Energy Circles (see page 101).

6

Further Techniques

Switchwords, tapping and NLP

Tapping, also known as Emotional Freedom Techniques (EFTs), involves tapping on eight acupoints on the body or fingers in sequence while saying aloud a phrase that describes a problem and its associated feelings. Recent research at Harvard University, along with other studies, have shown that stimulating certain meridian acupoints calms the part of the brain responsible for the fear response. Tapping has had lots of success treating phobias, post-traumatic stress disorder, performance anxiety, physical pain and addiction, helping people quit smoking and lose weight. It's based on Thought Field Therapy, a technique developed by Dr Roger Callahan, which desensitises a problem through exposure, or 'reverse psychology'. In traditional tapping, a problem is repeated out loud so the brain recategorises it as less threatening or non-threatening. During the tapping process, hidden issues connected with the problem may surface, so they can be cleared from the energy system.

Tapping, because it affects the subconscious mind, is also an effective way to 'tap in' positive words – a perfect pathway for Switchwords.

There are eight tapping points on the body, and four on the fingers. You can tap on the body if it's convenient, or you may prefer to finger-tap (which you can do discreetly when travelling or in any other public space). Tapping takes only a few moments, and some people love this technique because the tapping action keeps the conscious mind busy and distracted with an action, while the Switchwords get to work on conditioning the subconscious mind to activate a goal.

We begin tapping in our Switchwords with what's termed a 'set-up statement' – a phrase that sums up our situation and helps remove any negative self-talk or judgement around the request. When this is done, we work our way through the tapping points, saying or intending the Switchword at each point – you don't need to say any other words. Just recite the Switchword, and tap. (To explore the tapping process in more depth, see Further Reading and Research on page 147.)

Tapping points on the body

1 The karate-chop point on the fleshy side of the hand
2 The eyebrow – the inner point, around where the eyebrow begins
3 Side of eye – between the outer point of the eye and the temple
4 Under the eye – on the cheekbone, in line with the pupil of the eye
5 Under the nose – between the nose and the top lip
6 The chin – in the chin indent
7 The collarbone – just under the collarbone, towards the neck
8 Under the arm – around 4 inches under the arm; on women, where the lower bra strap would be
9 Top of the head

Finger-tapping points

1 Side of thumb
2 Side of index finger
3 Side of middle finger
4 Side of little finger

   (Note: We don't use the ring finger for finger-tapping, but if you forget not to tap here, it's fine – it just isn't effective.)

How to tap in your Switchword

- Begin by identifying the Switchword that represents what you want. In this example we will use the money Switchword COUNT.
- Tap on the karate-chop point and say a 'set-up statement' out loud: 'Even though I [have this problem/am in this situation/have this desire], I completely accept myself.' So this might be: 'Even though I need money at the moment, I completely accept myself.' Say the set-up statement three times as you tap five to seven times on the karate-chop point.
- Now tap in your Switchword on each of the eight tapping points on your body, or on the four points on your fingers. Say the word out loud or silently as you tap five to seven times on each point. For example:
  Eyebrow: COUNT
  Under eye: COUNT
  Under nose: COUNT
  Chin: COUNT
  Collarbone COUNT
  Under arm: COUNT
  Top of head: COUNT

Or if using finger-tapping points:
    Side of thumb: COUNT
    Side of index finger: COUNT
    Side of middle finger: COUNT
    Side of little finger: COUNT

Take a breath, and repeat twice more.

Sian's Switchword tapping for exam panic

One of my clients, Sian, had a presentation coming up, during which she would have to address a room of around 50 delegates for the first time. The thought of it was sending her into a tailspin. 'Every time I try to plan out my talk, or practise, I just get a block, because I think I'm going to fail,' she confessed. Sian had successfully used tapping (without Switchwords) before to help with migraines, and now was willing to try tapping in Switchwords to calm her dread of failure. She chose TOGETHER ('This word makes me feel calmer') and GOLD, for thriving under pressure, and said TOGETHER-GOLD while she tapped on her fingers. After three rounds of Switch-tapping, she began to feel a bit more confident. When the presentation came around, an hour beforehand she tapped the 'orator's' Switchword ACT to get her in the mood for public speaking – and with the block of failure gone, she took to the stage, began to talk and her words flowed.

NLP: Empowering your Switchwords with images

Say these words: CURVE, TINY, SWING. Instantly you generate an image. The image connects us with our subconscious and the right side of the brain, the hemisphere that deals in feelings, pictures and intuition. CURVE might be a crescent moon; TINY, a small toy; SWING, a tennis player returning a serve. These are purely my images, and yours may be different. We're not in control of them; when we say a Switchword, they arise spontaneously from the sub-conscious mind. What's interesting, though, is becoming aware of these images so that we begin to forge a connection between the image and the word. When you use Switchwords regularly and you're familiar with them, you may find that the image comes almost before the word (as light travels faster than sound). For REACH, a common image is seeing a hand reach upwards – which may pop into your mind before you've finished thinking or saying the word.

Switchwords and NLP

NLP, or neuro-linguistic programming, is a form of therapy that uses words and images to clear unwanted beliefs and behaviours. Therapists use visualisation, movement and language techniques with their clients to effect positive change. While Switchwords are not based on NLP, there are similarities in approach – NLP has its own set of 'magic words' used during therapy, some of which are employed in marketing and advertising strategies to elicit an emotional response to a product or a bond with a buyer. NLP magic words include 'remarkable', 'secret', 'inspires', 'take', 'you', 'improvement', 'amazing', 'free', 'because', 'help', 'promote', 'increase', 'create', 'discover', 'now', 'instantly', 'new', 'naturally' and 'aware'. Coincidentally, 'take', 'amazing', 'help', 'create', 'discover' and 'new' are also Switchwords.

Visualisation techniques are a core part of NLP practice. If we consider that Switchwords use specific vocabulary that often conjures an image (and Switchwords can be defined as 'one-word visualisations'), there's certainly an affinity between NLP and Switchwords, in that they share the fundamental belief that words and images, used in a specific way, can create lasting change.

NLP practitioner Christina related how she combined NLP for herself with Switchwords as follows:

Christina's NLP Switchwording to stop overthinking

Christina explained to me how she had tried OFF to get to sleep (see page 78), but wasn't seeing the results she wanted because, as she told me, 'my brain is just so busy when I get to bed I can't stop my thoughts, and I was trying to say OFF, but it just didn't feel like it was registering. I wanted to stop my thoughts and it felt like STOP might help me with the over-thinking. So I visualised the "stop" traffic sign and repeated STOP to myself – and I suddenly found I'd stopped those thoughts. I began to breathe differently, something kind of peaceful stepped in – and I slept. Sometimes I use STOP then OFF to get to sleep quickly, other times STOP works just fine on its own.'

Christina also played with her stop-sign image. She'd done this many times, as it was part of her NLP training, so she felt comfortable working with mental images. 'I made the sign bigger, bringing it towards me, and saw that my thoughts were showing up as a kind of grey cloud that blurred then receded into the background. The closer I brought my stop sign, the more the thought-clouds moved back. The word "stop" became sharper and brighter, and as soon as the sign couldn't get any closer to me, that was it – the visualisation of my personal Switchword had worked.'

Using visualisation with Switchwords empowers our practice, because we're investing the word with emotion and imagination – two attributes of the subconscious mind. Through the senses, we're communicating a powerful message to the universe to bring us what we're asking for.

💡 Try this: Imagining with Switchwords

1 Choose your Switchword.

2 Close your eyes and take one deep breath.

3 Visualise the word – see it on a billboard, a traffic sign, a placard or as a tattoo. Paint the word on canvas with a paintbrush, see yourself hand-writing it on a card or typing it large in an email.

4 Play with the presentation. Experiment with making the word bigger and smaller. Can you feel the difference?

5 Now give the image some impact. Add a vivid colour to the letters, give them an orange or yellow glow, add highlights or another outline around the letter shapes. Make the word as intense and colourful as you can. Make it bigger and brighter. As you intensify the image, you activate an emotional response to the word; your subconscious mind is really taking notice.

6 Now lock onto that image. Feel it impress on your memory.

When you next use this Switchword, you'll find this image naturally arises with it.

Appendices

I ⟩ The Origins of Switchwords

Switchwords – today's words of magic – were devised by James T. Mangan, although for the origins of the word, we first turn to Freud.

The term 'switch-word' was first mentioned by Freud in 1905 in his 'Fragment of an Analysis of a Case of Hysteria': 'In a line of associations, ambiguous words (or, as we may call them, 'switch-words') act like points at a junction. If the points are switched across from the position in which they appear to lie in the dream, then we find ourselves on another set of rails, and along this second track run the thoughts which we are in search of but which still lie concealed beneath the dream.'

The context of Freud's comments is his interpretations of the dreams of his patient, Dora, in which she talks of a jewel case, which Freud posits as a sexual symbol – the word is a switch, a node or verbal bridge that carries a literal and covert meaning. French psychoanalyst Jacques Lacan, in *Écrits* (1977), suggests a possible benefit of these 'switch-words', in that they might be considered a type of metaphor to help remove 'stressful psychological conflict', leading to a 'switch in attention'. Yet, since the 1960s, a unique system of Switchwords has been in circulation, identified not by a psychologist, but created by an advertising executive from Illinois.

Switchwords, as they are used today and introduced in parts of this book, were the brainchild of James T. Mangan (1896–1970), a motivational author, advertising executive and entrepreneur. According to his grandson Dean Stump, in 1948 Mangan was in his Chicago office discussing with his colleague Everett Eckland ESP (extra-sensory perception) and how thoughts could travel through space when Mangan commented, 'I wonder who owns it?' At that point, Mangan founded the Nation of Celestial Space and claimed ownership of outer space. 'A new, bold, immodest idea,' he told *Science Illustrated* in 1949, and revealed his plans, eventually, to sell pieces of space the size of the earth for a dollar apiece, although he quickly realised that this was untenable. When his claim for the Nation of Celestial Space, or Celestia, was not acknowledged, he applied for a seat on the United Nations, claiming 100,000 supporters. Mangan also believed his nation would give people a more peaceful perspective, and he aimed to become a guardian for outer space, speaking out against weapons in space and promoting space travel, amongst many other things. 'If you owned something 8,000 miles in diameter and 25,000 miles in circumference, you might realise that war is something to be laughed at,' he stated. 'My nation might even give people enough bigness of thinking, enough bigness of disdain to make them feel international squabbles are petty.' Mangan's determination to officially establish Celestia saw him have passports and coins produced, one of which shows the head of his daughter, Ruth Mangan, as the allegorical figure Magnanimity. Magnanimity is also one of Mangan's Switchwords (see the Switchword Dictionary on page 131), recited to encourage generosity and stop petty attitudes.

Mangan's list of Switchwords appears in his 1963 book *The Secret of Perfect Living*, in which he sets out a philosophy of personal success based on the idea that a single word can switch on the machine of the subconscious to effect positive change. It is not known if Mangan himself was aware of Freud's use of the term 'switch-word', but Freud's comment does suggest the possibility of a language of the subconscious that Mangan identified and refined. Over 45 years, Mangan researched the four principles and the Switchwords presented in his landmark book.

James T. Mangan and New Thought

Mangan's book may be considered part of the New Thought movement established in the late 1800s, which proposed that thought, meditation and prayer could create the better reality we deserve.

Through self-belief and dissolving emotional blocks, we could get rich and be successful – a concept we're still enchanted by today, evidenced by the international success of Rhonda Byrne's film and book *The Secret* (2006). Three notable titles inspired *The Secret*: Wallace D. Wattles's *The Science of Getting Rich* (1910), Robert Collier's *The Secret of the Ages* (1926) and Charles Haanel's *The Master Key System* (1916), which states: 'We create our own character, personality and environment by the thought which we originate, or entertain ... Mental currents are as real as electric, magnetic or heat currents. We attract the currents with which we are in harmony.' This is the Law of Attraction, the guiding principle of *The Secret*: that like attracts like. Create a vibration through your thoughts, and you attract and receive the same quality of experience. Life responds in kind to your wishes. So the more positive the thought and the belief behind it, the more the abundance materialises. When our thoughts vibrate at the resonance of the experience of the wish, the wish comes true. In order to manifest successfully, we need to believe in the outcome and actually feel as if it has already happened. We create the reality we want through thought-power, sending our wish to a receptive, benevolent universe that wants to bring us the abundance we all deserve. Within this concept is the belief that the universe has to be alive if it is to respond to us.

In *The Secret of Perfect Living*, Mangan describes how he found 'a one-word formula for everything' on 10 March 1951, when 'a word fell out of the sky and into my arms ... The word seemed to be alive, and like a living spirit; it said confidently and unmistakably, "I am the HOW in 'How to achieve happiness on this earth.'"' The word was the familiar, supremely obvious word: "TOGETHER".

'I began saying TOGETHER to myself quietly, easily, without command. No exclamation point followed it, and no verb or adjective was connected with it. TOGETHER. Nothing else. TOGETHER. Then a pause. Then — TOGETHER ... After half a century of fighting with myself, wrestling with myself on every little problem and decision, I suddenly found myself *on my own side ...*'

Mangan's experience of self-togetherness during the week that followed proved, to him, 'that the best way for the conscious mind of you and me to communicate with our subconscious sides was through the medium of a *single word*'.

Mangan's language in *The Secret of Perfect Living* echoes that of the pioneer New Thoughters. Charles Haanel's *The Master Key System* and Mangan's description of Switchwords as 'a key for every lock' both suggest approaching the body and mind as a machine that can be made to work more effectively through thought- and word-power. As in Mangan's *Perfect Living*, the emphasis in the books published during his lifetime is on unlocking the subconscious as the key to success. As Freud's case studies explored the recesses of the subconscious, New Thought writers such as Mangan sought to unleash the innate power of the subconscious within us all.

The language of persuasion

Mangan's Switchword list, which appears in *The Secret of Perfect Living*, has an additional context, alongside New Thought: the rise of advertising in the 1950s and 1960s. In Mangan's list of Switchwords (see the Switchword Dictionary on page 131), it's notable that the words reflect the economic landscape of his era, as perhaps one would expect. The 1950s saw the prosperity boom in America, and the growth of popular culture through the relatively new medium of television, through which ad men and women could sell a product on the back of the new American dream of perfection in suburbia. This desire for upward social mobility is reflected in a number of Mangan's Switchwords: CLASSIC, to appear cultured; WASTE, to appear wealthy; TAP, to convert; and, as an advertising executive himself, the word RIDICULOUS, 'to secure publicity'.

As Mangan continued to research Switchwords 'on thousands of experiments on people from all walks of life' to help them live the lives they wanted, so the advertising industry noted the most effective power-words for selling to the public. In 1963, the same year as the publication of Mangan's *The Secret of Perfect Living*, ad supremo and 'father of advertising' David Ogilvy presented in his first book, *Confessions of an Advertising Man*, his list of the 22 most influential single words in headline copy. Out of his list, eight are also Switchwords: 'suddenly', 'now', 'amazing', 'miracle', 'magic', 'offer', 'free' and 'easy' (the Switchword is EASE). Identifying the words that switched on the public's desire to buy was profitable research.

Beyond Mangan

Mangan's Switchword legacy after his death in 1970 was continued by Shunyam Nirav, who in 1975 found Mangan's *The Secret of Perfect Living*, then out of print, in a bookstore in California. Nirav, a writer, artist and musician, was so inspired that he went on to research Switchwords for the next 30 years, teaching through his Switchword group and his book, *Switchwords Easily Give to You Whatever You Want in Life*. Nirav's book aimed to continue and update Mangan's, making it relevant for contemporary readers; he added over 20 new Switches and included the majority of Mangan's list. Like Mangan, a selection of the Switchwords he includes are cultural echoes of his world, such as LOVE (to attract love) and ZEN (to get into a meditative state). Nirav died in March 2008, but his work on Switchwords was continued by Kat Miller, who had joined Nirav's Yahoo Switchwords group around the time that Nirav became ill and had to limit his time running it. She became the group's moderator and eventually took over when Nirav passed on. Since then, Kat and other Switchword researchers have continued to publish new experimental Switchwords on their blogs and websites, sharing the special gift of word-manifesting with us all.

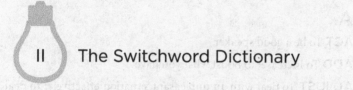

II The Switchword Dictionary

Traditionally, there are three types of Switchword: universal, open and personal, to which I have added an additional category of experimental. Experimental Switchwords, which carry an asterisk in the list below, are new Switches researched for this book. Personal Switchwords are those that have resonance for you; there is space left at the end of this list to write these in, so you can record the date and the results they bring (see Chapter 4).

Universal Switchwords are shown in bold underlined for those listed in James T. Mangan's book *The Secret of Perfect Living*, and in bold italics for those listed in Shunyam Nirav's *Switchwords Easily Give You Whatever You Want in Life* and those included in ongoing Switchword research by Kat Miller and others. According to Mangan and Nirav's research, universal Switchwords work for 95–100 per cent of people.

Open Switchwords, which are in plain text, flip switches in 50–94 per cent of people. There are many open Switchwords in circulation that are believed to work for most people. Those shown below are a selection that evolved from flower-remedy names and from the research of Kat Miller. (For further Switchword lists, see Kat Miller's excellent websites in Further Reading and Research on page 147.)

A

ACT To be a good speaker

ADD To increase; to boost what you have

ADJUST To deal with an unpleasant situation effectively; to deal with a responsibility or burden

AGRIMONY Flower-remedy Switch; reduces oversensitivity (see page 107)

*ANGEL For guidance

ALERT To increase awareness and be mindful

ALL IN To completely enjoy, embrace and absorb with total certainty; a miraculous, multi-level breakthrough

ALLOW To access or release; to discover

ALONE To heal a scab; generally, to promote healing

AROUND For better perspective

ASPEN Flower-remedy Switch; reduces fear (see page 108)

ATTENTION To pay attention to detail; to avoid careless mistakes

B

*BEACH To dream, to relax and stretch out

BETWEEN To discover or boost psychic ability; to enhance telepathy

BE To have good health; to be resilient to ridicule and other negative attitudes; to feel less alone; for peace of mind; to do well at sport

BEECH Flower-remedy Switch; reduces overcare and concern (see page 108)

BINGO To feel excited; to win; to get it right

BLUFF To reduce or dispel anxiety, fear or nervousness

BOW For humility; to stop arrogance; to make something smaller

BREAKTHROUGH To discover; to innovate

BRING For motivation; for pregnancy; to manifest or deliver

BUBBLE For energy and excitement; to go beyond perceived limitations

C

<u>CANCEL</u> To dispel worry, poverty, debt, annoyance, negativity or any unwanted condition

<u>CARE</u> To remember; to retain information

CATALYST To trigger a reaction; to bring on change

CENTAURY Flower-remedy Switch; reduces oversensitivity (see page 107)

CERATO Flower-remedy Switch; reduces uncertainty (see page 109)

*CHAMPION To back a winner; to find a good investment

<u>CHANGE</u> To get rid of pain in any part of the body, or anything else unwanted, such as negative thoughts; to get something out of the eye

CHARM To manifest your heart's desire

CHERRY PLUM Flower-remedy Switch; reduces fear (see page 108)

CHESTNUT BUD Flower-remedy Switch; reduces apathy (see page 111)

CHICORY Flower-remedy Switch; reduces overcare and concern (see page 109)

CHLORINE To socialise and mingle; to make a difference; to blend; to become one with

<u>CHUCKLE</u> For personal confidence; to turn on personality

CIRCULATE To banish loneliness and boost social life

CLASSIC To appear cultured

CLEAR To clear negativity and neutralise anger

CLEMATIS Flower-remedy Switch; reduces apathy (see page 111)

CLIMB To rise; to enhance your viewpoint

COMPASSION To be kind and accepting; to alleviate pain

CONCEDE To stop quarrels

CONDUIT To find a path; to deliver or communicate

CONFESS To end aggression

CONTINUE To increase endurance; to swim

CONSIDER To be a good mechanic; to diagnose

COPY To have good taste; to boost fertility

*CORN For abundance

COUNT To make money; to cut down smoking

COVER To subdue excitement; to calm nerves

CRAB APPLE Flower-remedy Switch; reduces apathy (see page 111)

CRISP To revitalise; to enhance

CROWD To get your children to follow orders

*CROWN For success and acknowledgement; for ambition and self-direction

CRYSTAL For clarity; to look to the future; to improve clairvoyance; to purify; to neutralise; to access Universal Knowledge

*CRYSTAL To attune the third eye chakra; to support intuition

CURVE To make beautiful; to create an item of beauty; for self-esteem

CUT To moderate behaviour; to curb excesses

D

DEACTIVATION To make inactive; to calm

DEDICATE To stop clinging

DIVINE To work miracles; to enhance your strengths

DIVINE LIGHT To intensify; to increase enlightenment and focus positivity

DIVINE ORDER To put in order or repair; to be organised and efficient; to tidy; to help pack; to garden; to tune a musical instrument

DIVINE TIMING To speed up or bring forward an event if this is right for the person making the request

DO To beat procrastination

DONE To meet a deadline; to boost willpower

DOWN For humility; to stop bragging

DUCK To reduce hypersensitivity

E

ELATE To turn a setback to your advantage

ENVELOPE To wrap; to make secure; to prioritise

*ENVELOPE To ask for protection

ENGAGE To be with possibilities; to fill a space; to hold attention

ELM Flower-remedy Switch; reduces apathy (see page 112)

F

FIGHT To win in a competition, such as a sports match; to upset an opponent

FIND To amass a fortune

FLOWER To open up; to flourish

FOR To promote

FOREVER To keep a secret

FORGIVE To forgive; to end resentment or the need for revenge

G

GENTIAN Flower-remedy Switch; reduces uncertainty (see page 110)

GIGGLE To get in the mood for writing

GIVE To sell and to be generous; to be a helper

GO To stop being lazy

*GOLD To thrive under pressure

GORSE Flower-remedy Switch; reduces uncertainty (see page 109)

GUARD To protect personal space or property

GUESS To stop overthinking and procrastinating

H

HALFWAY To cut down a journey time; to make a goal less arduous

HAVEN To feel safe; to create opportunities

HEATHER Flower-remedy Switch; reduces loneliness (see page 112)

HELP To stop procrastination and uncertainty

HO To sigh; to relax

HOLD To maximise positive character traits

*HOLD To keep your personal boundaries if feeling compromised

HOLE To boost charisma; to be attractive

HOLLY Flower-remedy Switch; reduces oversensitivity (see page 107)

HOME To find a home or create one

*HOME To attune the root or base chakra; to feel more secure and grounded

HONEYSUCKLE Flower-remedy Switch; reduces apathy (see page 111)

HORNBEAM Flower-remedy Switch; reduces uncertainty (see page 110)

HORSE For power and strength

*HUM To align all the chakras (Julie Leivers' Switchword, see page 97)

I

*I AM In healing, to attune the throat chakra; to boost self-expression; to find truth

IMPATIENS Flower-remedy Switch; reduces loneliness (see page 112)

J

*JEWEL In healing, to attune the solar plexus chakra; to reduce fear

JUDGE To enjoy reading; to help work and study; to improve understanding

L

LARCH Flower-remedy switch; reduces despondency and despair (see page 112)

LAVENDER To help relax and sleep

LEARN For an instant youthful attitude and appearance

*LENNON To reconcile; to find love and peace

LIGHT For inspiration; to lighten mood

*LIGHT To bring healing light

LISTEN To predict the future

LOVE To attract and generate love

*LOVE To attune the heart chakra; to heal the emotions

M

*ME Privacy; time for me

MAGNANIMITY For generosity; to stop petty attitudes

MASK To protect, to shield

MONA LISA To smile; to dispel hate or envy

MOVE For sudden energy

MIMULUS Flower-remedy Switch; reduces fear (see page 108)

MUSIC To flow in harmony, with love

MUSTARD Flower-remedy Switch; reduces uncertainty (see page 110)

N

NEXT To complete a detailed, repetitive task, such as accounts, domestic work or exam revision

NOW To act on a positive impulse or idea; to beat procrastination

O

OAK Flower-remedy Switch; reduces despondency and despair (see page 112)

*OCEAN To dream

OFF To get to sleep or break a bad habit; the 'quit' Switch

OFFER To suppress greed

OLIVE Flower-remedy Switch; reduces uncertainty (see page 110)

ON The 'green-light' Switchword; to get new ideas and to travel; to be ambitious; to build, create or produce

OPEN To open up to inspiration; to connect; to comprehend

*OPEN In healing, to open up the chakras

OVER To end frustration

OWL To see new perspectives; to notice subtle differences

P

PERSONAL To publish a successful website, newsletter or blog

PINE Flower-remedy Switch; reduces despondency and despair (see page 113)

PHASE To set goals, routine or pattern; to improve a situation

PLENTY For abundance and generosity

POINT To improve eyesight

POSTPONE To stop a sulk

PRAISE To make yourself beautiful or handsome; to like your body; to get praise from others; to stop finding fault in others

*PURE To attune the crown chakra; for spiritual connection

PURGE To purge; to cancel

PUT To build or develop

Q

QUIET To subdue the ego

R

REACH The 'lightbulb' Switch: to find lost objects; to remember; to be creative and invent; to find inspiration; to solve problems; to find the right words

RED CHESTNUT Flower-remedy Switch; reduces fear (see page 108)

REJOICE To stop being jealous

RELEASE To have charisma

RESTORE To rebalance; to bring justice; restores what you feel you have lost

REVERSE To bury a grudge; to move on

RIDICULOUS To promote successfully; to get publicity

ROCK ROSE Flower-remedy Switch; reduces fear (see page 108)

ROCK WATER Flower-remedy Switch; reduces overcare and concern (see page 109)

*ROOM To relax; to switch off

ROOT To dig; discover; grow

*ROOT In healing, to feel grounded

S

SAGE To dispel negative energies

SAVE To stop drinking

SCHEME To design; to advertise; to produce

SCLERANTHUS Flower-remedy Switch; reduces uncertainty (see page 110)

*SHINE To bless; to raise the vibration; to lift a mood; to clear negativity; to attract special attention

SHOW To be sincere; to be devout

SHUT To stop looking for trouble

SING To trigger emotion; to feel the impact of words

SLOW To have patience and wisdom

SMILE To smile

SOPHISTICATE To publish a successful magazine; to increase success

SPEND To dress well; to improve appearance

*STICK To hold attention; to concentrate

STAR OF BETHLEHEM Flower-remedy Switch; reduces despondency and despair (see page 113)

*STOP To stop overthinking; to promote sleep

STRETCH To sustain a good feeling or situation; to prolong a winning streak

SUFFER To manage success and prosperity

SWEET To be a calming influence; to be good company

*SWEET To attune the sacral chakra; to remove blocks to creativity/fertility

SWEET CHESTNUT Flower-remedy Switch; reduces despondency and despair (see page 113)

SWING For courage; to confront a situation

SWIVEL To relieve constipation

T

TAKE To cultivate leadership

TAP To convert or persuade someone

THANKS To stop regretting the past

*THANKYOU Thanks to the powers that be (Julie Leivers)

TINY To be kind, polite and considerate

TOGETHER The master Switchword: brings whatever you want; aligns the subconscious and conscious selves as one

TOMORROW To stop remorse

TRANSFORM To improve; to bring positive change; to make progress

*TURN To turn anything around; to transform negatives to positives

U

UNCLE To retain sense of self when first feeling a negative influence

UP For confidence; to lose an inferiority complex; to dispel a low mood

V

VERVAIN Flower-remedy Switch; reduces overcare and concern (see page 109)

VINE Flower-remedy Switch; reduces overcare and concern (see page 109)

W

WAIT To learn a secret

WALNUT Flower-remedy Switch; reduces oversensitivity (see page 107)

WASTE To appear wealthy

WATCH To learn a skill

WATER VIOLET Flower-remedy Switch; reduces loneliness (see page 112)

WHITE CHESTNUT Flower-remedy Switch; reduces apathy (see page 111)

WILD OAT Flower-remedy Switch; reduces uncertainty (see page 110)

WILD ROSE Flower-remedy Switch; reduces apathy (see page 111)

WILLOW Flower-remedy Switch; reduces despondency and despair (see page 113)

WIND To access your hidden power

WINDFALL For an immediate win, payout or bonus; for an increase in wealth

WINGS To rise above pressure or pain; to move freely

WITH For compatibility; to get on with other people

WOLF For stamina; for strong decisions; for social confidence

WOMB To feel nurtured; to be cuddly; to feel secure; to reconnect with the Source

*WRAP To secure; to ask for protection

Y

YES! To motivate; to stop procrastination

Z

ZEN To get into a meditative state

Date	Personal Switchword	Notes

| Date | Personal Switchword | Notes |

| Date | Personal Switchword | Notes |

Further Reading and Research

Kat Miller
   http://blueiris.org/community/
   http://www.powerfulintentions.org/profile/KatMiller

Doron Alon, *Switchword Miracles: Creating Miracles, One Word at a Time* (Numinosity Press, 2012)

Sue Beer, Emma Roberts, *Step-by-Step Tapping: The Amazing Self-Help Technique* (Gaia, 2013)

James T. Mangan, *The Secret of Perfect Living* (Infinity Publishing, reprint edition 2006)

Shunyam Nirav, *Switchwords Easily Give to You Whatever You Want in Life* (Masterworks Unlimited, 2006)

Natasha Williams, *Switchword Magic: The Secret to Getting Everything You Want in Life* (New Concept Media, 2014)

Chapter references

Introduction

Ali Baba and the Forty Thieves, retold excerpt, Liz Dean

Meme theory: *The Selfish Gene*, Richard Dawkins (OUP, 2006)

Switchwords as mantra: Dr Douglas Brookes on Sanskrit: http://health. usnews.com

Why Switchwords succeed where affirmations can fail: Mark Waldman and Andrew Newberg MD, 'The most dangerous word in the world', *Psychology Today* (1 August 2012)

Chapter 1

The subconscious has impeccable timing: Heather A. Berlin, 'The Neural Basis of the Dynamic Unconscious', Neuropsychoanalysis 13 (1) (2011)

5 per cent/95 per cent: Marianne Szegedy-Maszak, 'Mysteries of the mind: Your unconscious is making your everyday decisions', US News and World Report/Auburn University

What the subconscious learns at night school: Bruce H. Lipton PhD, *The Biology of Belief: Unleashing the power of consciousness, matter and miracles* (Hay House, 2008)

Northwestern University research: Gordon B. Feld and Jan Born, 'Unlearning implicit social biases during sleep', *Science*, vol. 348, no. 6238 (29 May 2015), pp. 1013–1015

Recognising self-conflict: 'neurons that fire together, wire together' is a summarisation of Hebbian theory. The phrase, summarising the theory, is credited to neuroscientist Carla Shatz.

Dealing with shame: Jon Ronson, *So You've Been Publicly Shamed* (Picador, 2015)

Chapter 3

Creative problem-solving – BRING: Isaiah Hankel, *Black Hole Focus: How intelligent people can create a powerful purpose for their lives* (Capstone, 2014)

Personal Empowerment – MONA LISA: Andrew Newberg MD and Mark Robert Waldman, *Words Can Change Your Brain: 12 conversation strategies to build trust, resolve conflict and increase intimacy* (Penguin, 2014)

Sales, promotion and marketing – RIDICULOUS: Diane Boerstler, MNlp, www.nlphypnocopy.com

Managing pain – CHANGE: Caroline Myss PhD, *Why People Don't Heal and How They Can: A practical programme for healing body, mind and spirit* (Bantam, 1998)

Chapter 5

Chakra Switchwords: Dr David Shannahoff-Khalsa on mantra repetition: http://www.wakingtimes.com

Attuning water with Switchwords: Dr Masaru Emoto, *The Hidden Messages in Water* (Beyond Words Publishing, 2004) and http://www.masaru-emoto.net

Solfeggio scale numbers: Dr Leonard G. Horowitz and Dr Joseph S. Puleo, *Healing Codes for the Biological Apocalypse* (Healthy World, 1999)

Appendices: I. The Origin of Switchwords

Origin of 'Switchword': Sigmund Freud, 'Fragment of an Analysis of a Case of Hysteria' (1905) in *Dora: An Analysis of a Case of Hysteria* (Touchstone, 1997)

Switchwords as metaphor: Jacques Lacan, *Écrits: The First Complete Edition in English* (W. W. Norton, 2007)

James T. Mangan: Dean Stump, preface to James T. Mangan's *The Secret of Perfect Living* (Infinity Publishing, 2006; reprint of the 1963 edition)

Mangan and Celestia: 'Chicago Man Stakes Claim to Outer Space', *Science Illustrated* (May 1949); and https://en.wikipedia.org/wiki/Nation_of_Celestial_Space

Mangan and advertising: David Ogilvy, *Confessions of an Advertising Man* (Southbank Publishing, 2004; first published 1963)

Index

Acknowledgements

The following people have been invaluable in their support: First and foremost, Michael Young, for insight, love and support; and Jennifer Hykin, Claire Gillman, Kathy Hulme, Christina Archbold, Steve Jex, Rhonda Mason, Tania O'Donnell, Mary Lambert, Mary Young, Jayne Wallace, Eric and Jean Dean, Julia Dus, Kim Arnold, Yasia Williams-Leedham and Jackie Cox. Petra Galligan and Julie Leivers gave their time, expertise and energy researching the chakra Switches, and adding their own – I am deeply grateful. (To contact Petra Galligan, see Create and Connect on Facebook.) I give eternal thanks to Kat Miller for her kindness, her contribution on Energy Circles and for the inclusion of the Switchwords within this book that she has researched.

I also thank Diane Boerstler, MNlp, for Switchwords and hypnocopy: http://nlphypnocopy.com; and Dean Stump, the grandson of James T. Mangan, the creator of Switchwords, for checking the biographical detail of James Mangan's life.

Carolyn Thorne of HarperCollins and my agent, Chelsey Fox, receive a special award for believing wholeheartedly in this book.

ANGEL-LIGHT-DIVINE-THANKS.

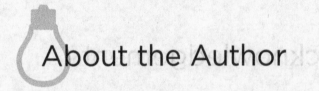

About the Author

Liz Dean is a former commissioning editor and author of fifteen books and card decks, which include *How to Be Creative* (Cico Books, 2015), *A Thousand Paths to Mindfulness* (Spruce, 2015), and *The Art of Tarot* (Cico Books, 2001), which has sold one-third of a million copies worldwide. She has run workshops in London on tarot and the creative process for writers and artists, and currently gives Angelic Reiki healing, reads cards and teaches creativity and angel tarot at Selfridges, London. Liz is a published poet and a former co-editor of the UK's leading spiritual magazine, *Kindred Spirit*.

www.lizdean.com

To join the Switchword conversation, see Liz's Switchword website: www.switchwordspower.com